Anna-Maria Bauer

111 Places in Winchester That You Shouldn't Miss

emons:

To Steve, who made England feel like home.

Cäcilienstraße 48, 50667 Köln
info@emons-verlag.de

Layout: Anja Sauerland, based on a design
by Lübbeke | Naumann | Thoben
Maps: altancicek.design, www.altancicek.de
Basic cartographical information from Openstreetmap,
© OpenStreetMap-Mitwirkende, OdbL
Edited by: Tania Taylor
Printing and binding: sourc-e GmbH
Printed in Europe 2026
ISBN 978-3-7408-2562-1
First edition

Guidebooks for Locals & Experienced Travellers
Join us in uncovering new places around the world at
www.111places.com

Foreword

Before I went to London for my year abroad at UCL, I had a naïvely romantic idea of the quintessential English countryside lifestyle. A Disney-fied version of small cottages with large bay windows and bellied teapots on cast-iron AGAs; of quaint restaurants in timber-framed houses and crackling flames dancing in stone fireplaces; of crooked trees and bent alleyways leading to hidden gems. An image that surely could not be a reality.

And then I travelled to Winchester with a friend from Austria as part of a south-of-England tour before our first trimester was due to begin. It was a mild day in September as we searched for Jane Austen's last home, followed Keats' autumnal walk along the River Itchen, peeked into the cathedral, and ate our cheese sandwiches sitting on a bench in Abbey Gardens. I was surprisingly melancholic when we boarded the bus to move on to Exeter, and vowed to come back soon.

It took me 10 years to return to Winchester, when in the winter of 2020, love brought me from my flat in Vienna to a little house in Hampshire. We had both matured by then, the city and I. Although 10 years are, of course, nothing in the lifetime of a city built by the Romans so, in truth, it was only I who had grown and, consequently, saw the city differently. Turning from the High Street, and stepping through the covered passage beneath the grey house next to the Buttercross to reach The Square, the picturesque scene I found – the little restaurants in the narrow houses, the fairy lights in the trees, the colourful boulders in front of the City Museum – was so beautiful, it made my heart ache.

As I set out to explore the city in the subsequent months after the Covid lockdown eased, I couldn't help but be impressed at the variety, the depth and the beauty of the places I discovered – places with stories so brimming with history, heritage and pioneering passion, I became eager to share them. I hope the ones I offer here might bring you as much joy as they continue to bring me.

111 Places

1 Alfred, The Greatest

Really the greatest of them all

While the first residents of Winchester arrived during the Iron Age and the Romans established the new town of Venta Belgarum at this site around A.D. 43, it was a Saxon king who was the city's most vital ruler. In 871, Alfred the Great was crowned King of Wessex at 21 years of age and subsequently established Winchester as his centre – not only rebuilding the city after the Dark Ages but also making it the first capital of England.

Alfred envisioned Winchester as the largest burh (a fortified market town) and the hub of his kingdom. He further used the royal palace as the centre of his administration and ordered a new grand cathedral to be built, which was completed by his son Edward after Alfred's death in 899.

Today, a larger-than-life statue of the ruler towers over Broadway. In 1899, to celebrate the ruler's millenary, the city was granted the right to erect a monumental sculpture of the nation's founder. The official unveiling two years later was so grand it even found its way into *The New York Times* on 21 September 1901, which read: 'The City of Winchester was in holiday garb for to-day's ceremony, business was stopped, and the main thoroughfares were lined with troops.' Thousands watched as the procession marched from Westgate down to Broadway.

Although there are a few statues of Alfred in the kingdom, none is as grand as the design of sculptor Hamo Thornycroft, who built a 17-foot bronze statue in one single cast and positioned it on two large blocks of Cornish granite. The statue, which shows an ideal Alfred (as there are no surviving portraits), is still believed to be one of the largest single bronze figure ever created in the United Kingdom. It depicts the ruler standing upright, holding a sword in his right hand but pointing it downward triumphantly as if to declare: I have finally secured peace – and brought prosperity to this city.

Address King Alfred the Great Statue, 65 The Broadway, SO23 9BE | Getting there A short walk from Winchester bus station | Hours Accessible 24 hours | Tip For a cosy pub experience, visit its namesake, The King Alfred, on Saxon Road.

2 Alfred's Brewery

Liquid Saxon bronze

For Steve Haigh, beer brewing is far more than the simple act of crafting an amber-coloured alcoholic beverage. It is a fusion of chemical reactions and refined culinary skills, a blend of traditional techniques and ever-improving processes. While he quickly grew tired of other professions, brewing never failed to captivate him.

Yet for years, as he commuted to work in nearby regions, there was one question he couldn't shake off: why was there no brewery in his hometown of Winchester? By 2012, the itch had grown too strong, and he took matters into his own hands. Steve found a small premises in the northeast of the city and bought the best equipment he could afford. His goal: to craft a brew that was rich in flavour but still light and refreshing – something to delight its drinker after a long, hard week.

Looking at a newspaper clipping from the early days, pinned against the wall of his office, Steve Haigh can't help but smile. 'We did it all wrong in the beginning,' he admits. 'And it was really hard work.' The turning point came as people – unaware of his business – began raving about an exquisite new local beer: Saxon Bronze Ale. By 2017, his brewery was so successful, he could move into a larger venue just off Easton Lane. With upgraded equipment, he was able to produce six times as much beer while maintaining consistently high quality.

Today, he not only offers his award-winning Saxon Bronze, but also a pale, an amber and a stronger ale. And while most of his barrels are delivered to local pubs, customers can also purchase cans or draught beer dispensers directly from the microbrewery. Yet Steve's goal goes beyond personal success. He has no intention of growing into a nationwide business; instead, he hopes to inspire others to start their own microbreweries: 'I would love it if there was a brewery in every town.'

Address Alfred's Brewery, 6, Winnall Farm Industrial Estate, Easton Lane, Winchester, SO23 0HA, alfredsbrewery.co.uk | Getting there A 13-minute walk from Winchester bus station | Hours By arrangement, see website for details | Tip If you would like to try Steve's Saxon Bronze Ale in a pub, visit The Black Boy, The Old Vine or The Queen Inn.

3 The Arc

Dancing, skating, creating

Standing in the tranquil entrance area of Winchester's cultural hub, it is hard to imagine that this space of reflection was at times filled with shrieking laughter, at others with theatrical sound effects. But indeed, this building has seen an unusually rich history of transformation.

In the 1830s, a group of Wintonian businessmen formed the Winchester Corn Exchange to finance and commission the trading of grain. In need of a suitable edifice, they approached the English architect Owen Brown Carter and, for £4,000 (approximately £500,000 in today's money), he realised a striking building of mustard-yellow and white ashlar on a formerly empty space next to the Theatre Royal. Its Tuscan-style portico was likely inspired by St Paul's Church in London's Covent Garden.

After initial success, the building ceased to serve its original purpose in the latter part of the 19th century, giving rise to a variety of uses. In 1906, it was transformed into a skating rink and, in 1915, converted into the Empire Corn Exchange theatre. Just two years later, it became a cinema, before reopening as the Regent Dance Hall in 1922, offering residents space for light dancing. In 1933, cinema screenings returned, only to be replaced by a public library three years later. The building was finally adopted by Hampshire County Council in 1974.

Today, the former Corn Exchange – now known as The Arc – is a cultural hub offering live music and theatre shows, art exhibitions and workshops, while also housing one of Hampshire's most frequented libraries, as well as a light-filled café. You can channel your inner muse when joining in at one of their life drawing lessons, crafting a Jane Austen-inspired candle or a mini clay vase – ideal for holding dried flower bouquets, perhaps with a hint of grain, bringing the Corn Exchange full circle.

Address The Arc, Jewry Street, Winchester, SO23 8SB, www.arcwinchester.org.uk | Getting there A 5-minute walk from Winchester railway station | Hours Mon–Sat 9.30am–5pm, Sun 11am–5pm | Tip For a delicious dinner, visit the delicate Brasserie Blanc just down the road.

4 Betty Mundy's Bottom

What, truly, is in a name

Places we want to visit often call to us for a reason – this can be a picturesque view, historical significance, or the promise of a particularly indulgent café. But then there are also places that intrigue us for a very simple yet powerful reason: their name. This is the case with a little wooded valley that goes by the name Betty Mundy's Bottom.

The best way to reach Betty Mundy's Bottom is to set off from Beacon Hill car park. Turn right onto the tarmac road but continue straight when it bends, on a sheltered track, onto South Downs Way. Follow this path for three quarters of a kilometre before turning left onto Monarch's Way and left again after a converted barn onto Wayfarer's Walk. Continue on this track for half a kilometre, passing Preshaw Wood on your right. As you reach a three-way junction, turn left once more onto a smaller track. Having passed a copse, turn right over a stile. As you enter a meadow, keep left and look out for another stile, pass a narrow woodland, and turn right to follow the field along the edge. Go through a metal gate, over another stile and walk down a field on the left-hand side. Now you have reached Betty Mundy's Bottom.

The origin of the name is unclear. And while it might be that the Romans called this patch *beati mundae*, which is Latin for 'the most beautiful place in the world', might it not be chillingly fitting if a woman called Betty Mundy lived here in a cottage? Some say she lured passing sailors into her house, murdering them and keeping their money. Others claim she was in business with a press gang: tempting local farmers who were then forced into the navy, for commission. Another myth saw her accused of witchcraft, which gave the locals a reason to burn down her cottage – but the gold they hoped to capture was nowhere to be found. Some places truly call to us because of the fantastical stories they tell.

Address Betty Mundy's Bottom, Southampton, SO32 1QF | Getting there A 25-minute walk from Beacon Hill car park | Hours Accessible 24 hours | Tip In need for a refreshment after the walk? The charming Shoe Inn pub in Exton is only a 10-minute drive away.

5 Bishop's Waltham Palace

Where kings wait and queens anticipate

Today, only ruins remain but during the Middle Ages the palace of Bishop's Waltham was a magnificent place – even by the critical standards of the powerful bishops of Winchester, who were, it should be remembered, among the wealthiest men in Europe. Built by Henry de Blois, grandson of William the Conqueror, in the 12th century and later remodelled by Bishop William of Wykeham, it was set in picturesque grounds, enclosed by a moat and featured an imposing three-storey building as well as a great hall with the finest windows. So refined was the palace's presentation, it repeatedly proved an appropriate location for the partly nervous, partly excited anticipation of English monarchy.

Was the weather finally better on 11 August 1415? Had the rain that had slowed preparations ceased? Did the birds sing as Henry V woke up for the last time in this very palace before making his way to the port of Southampton? From there, he would sail to France to besiege the French in the Battle of Agincourt.

More than a century later, another King Henry – this time King Henry VIII – travelled to Bishop's Waltham. In 1522, he met Holy Roman Emperor Charles V to sign the Treaty of Waltham, promising an allegiance against the common enemy across the Channel, France. And finally, as third time's a charm: when Henry's daughter Mary, and Charles' son Philip, were set to be betrothed in Winchester, it was once again the quaint palace southeast of Winchester that proved the appropriate venue for their first meeting – which occurred only two days later.

Yet, the palace's legacy was not to last. The royal cavaliers had to surrender it on 9 April 1644. Bishop Walter Curle (whose legacy endures on the walls of Winchester Cathedral as the Riddle of Curle's Passage) had taken refuge in the palace. He knew he had to escape in order to survive. Legend has it, he did so in a cart of rotting horse manure.

Address Bishop's Waltham Palace, 3 Station Road, Bishop's Waltham, SO32 1DH | Getting there Take bus 69 to The Square in Bishop's Waltham, then a 4-minute walk | Hours Grounds open daily Apr–Sep 10am–6pm, and Oct–Mar 10am–4pm | Tip Stop for a coffee and a cake at Josie's, the lovely, independent, family-run café in the village.

6 The Black Swan

Meet Sherlock Holmes here

Sherlock Holmes is, obviously, at home in the gaslit streets, foggy alleyways and imposing mansions of Victorian London. But now and again, during his fifty-six short stories and four novels, he enjoys the lush countryside and the soft coastline of Hampshire, too. After all, the idea of the genius private detective came to his creator, Sir Arthur Conan Doyle, when he set up his doctor's practice in Elm Grove, Southsea.

While the author usually refrains from referring to establishments with their original names, Conan Doyle makes an exception in 'The Adventure of the Copper Beeches'. When the governess Violet Hunter asks Sherlock Holmes and Dr Watson to meet her, she writes: 'Please be at the Black Swan Hotel at Winchester at midday to-morrow [it said]. Do come! I am at my wit's end — Hunter.'

Although Sir Arthur Conan Doyle knew the area well (he not only worked in Portsmouth but later owned a house in the New Forest as well), he does not entirely stick to geographic truths. As Sherlock Holmes and Dr Watson arrive at Winchester Railway Station from London Waterloo, Holmes remarks, 'Well, there is the tower of the cathedral, and we shall soon learn all that Miss Hunter has to tell.' It is, of course, not possible to see the cathedral from there. Nevertheless, they move on to the High Street and find the Black Swan to be 'an inn of repute' and in 'no distance from the station' – which is true enough; it is a nine-minute walk, to be precise.

The Black Swan was situated in 65 High Street. It does not exist any more; the house was demolished in 1935 when the road was widened. But if you look up at the corner of High Street and Southgate Street, above the Harvey Jones Kitchen branch, you see a reminder: the statue of a black swan, wearing a golden crown on its neck, its wings spread as if ready for take-off. The swan is a replica of the statue that once adorned the entrance of the hotel.

Address Black Swan Buildings, 5 Southgate Street, Winchester, SO23 9DT | Getting there A 9-minute walk from Winchester railway station | Hours Accessible 24 hours | Tip Sir Arthur Conan Doyle's final resting place is only a 30-minute car ride away. The grave, located in Minstead Cemetery in the New Forest, is easily recognisable by the pipes and magnifying glasses left by literary fans.

7 The Bollards

Making beauty out of the mundane

As you cross The Square, whether from the High Street towards the Cathedral or vice versa, and look towards The Old Vine – her gaze keeps following you. Though she doesn't move, her eyes track you wherever you stand, her mouth curled into a subtle smile – just as in the original. Leonardo da Vinci's famous painting the *Mona Lisa* isn't only found behind protective glass in The Louvre: you can also see it on the curved surface of a Winchester bollard. And it is not the only masterpiece honoured in this public space: more than three dozen bollards have been adorned with works by renowned artists like Matisse, Magritte and Mondrian.

In 2005, the painters Jenny Muncaster and Rachael Alexander, who run The Colour Factory, set out to inject life and colour into Winchester's then 'drab and dreary' street furniture. Initially, the city council granted them permission to paint five bollards – an initiative believed to be the first of its kind in the country – for the duration of the annual Hat Fair.

Painting with acrylic on an even surface is one thing but replicating complex artworks on the bent, textured surface of cast-iron bollards was entirely a different matter. Firstly, the weather needed to be right. 'Even a small drop of rain would make the work impossible,' Jenny says. Secondly, special paint that would not rust had to be used. Rachael adds: 'The paint is great, but it dries already on the brush. Even if you stopped for a little chat, you would have to remix it.'

However, the bollards were so well received by residents that Jenny and Rachael did not just avoid repainting them in black and white after the fair – they went on to paint numerous others, advised various cities across the UK and compiled a *Bollard Advice Manual*. Some even claim that Winchester's *Mona Lisa* bollard has now been photographed more often than the city's Cathedral!

Address The Bollards, The Square, Winchester, SO23 9EX | Getting there An 11-minute walk from Winchester railway station | Hours Accessible 24 hours | Tip If you are interested in paintings, pottery or jewellery – to purchase or to make – visit the brilliant Colour Factory on the edge of River Park (www.thecolourfactory.org.uk).

8 Bombay Sapphire Distillery

A tour of spirits

Which aroma can you detect? Predominantly, there is, of course, the earthy pine of juniper. Harvested at an altitude of more than 800 metres in the Tuscan hills. Then, something citrussy. This comes not only from the lemon peel, handpicked and sundried in Spain, but also the coriander seeds grown in Morocco and delivered, like the other 10 botanicals, to a quaint redbrick estate in rural Hampshire.

At Laverstoke Mill, 15 miles north of Winchester, Bombay Sapphire not only produces all of the bottles enjoyed around the world but also hosts around 50,000 guests a year. Starting in the turbine room, the loud swooshing of water beneath you reminds you that this building was once a paper mill, producing bank notes under the reign of Queen Victoria. These days, the hydro-electric turbine generates enough power for the majority of the lighting.

Having created your first gin and tonic, you are invited into the world of Bombay Sapphire: to study samples of the 10 botanicals, marvel at Thomas Heatherwick's spectacular curved greenhouses and admire the two giant stills – Thomas and Mary – named after the recipe's founders, who helped pioneer the distillation process. While the traditional method involves soaking and then boiling botanicals in spirit, Bombay Sapphire uses vapour infusion. Here, the spirit is boiled beneath a perforated basket, containing the botanicals. As the alcohol vapour passes through as it rises, it gently extracts the aromatic oils and flavours, creating a softer, more delicate spirit... One that now begs to be sampled in a cocktail. How about a Bombay Sapphire, the drink brand ambassador Sam Carter invented for the venue? Following his instruction, a glass is filled with lime juice and ginger strips, before the gin is mixed with elderflower liqueur and Martini Bianco. A bouquet of sweet-sharp notes hits the nose, followed by the realisation that perhaps the late Queen Mother's habit of enjoying a gin before lunch deserves reconsideration. After all, she did live to 101.

Address Bombay Sapphire Distillery, Laverstoke Mill, London Road, Whitchurch, RG28 7NR, www.bombaysapphire.com/distillery | Getting there Take the train to Basingstoke, then bus 76 to Laverstoke Mill | Hours Advance booking required | Tip Want to see more of the countryside around Whitchurch? Follow the Watership Down Trail to explore the landscape immortalised in Richard Adams' classic novel.

9 Boys with Kite

How Hendog's art transforms the south coast

In March 2021, Winchester's wall became more alive. Overnight, the image of a little boy, holding a rainbow-coloured kite, had appeared on the brick bridge wall near the Handlebar Café on Garnier Road in St Cross. A delicate and detailed black-and-white illustration of a child with determined concentration on his face; an image that might evoke the soothing, yet aching memory of one's own childhood. 'I call it joyful nostalgia,' explains its creator, the street artist Hendog. 'I like to imagine that a piece of my art might catch a person on their commute to work or on their afternoon walk and offer them a moment of comfort.'

But is he not afraid, sneaking through dark streets at night with spray-paint and stencil in hand to bring a childhood scene to life on a public wall? 'Oh, yes, very much so,' he says. There is the constant threat of arrest, the worry of people stumbling upon him in the dark. But the fear was part of what drew him to start the project in the first place. 'I had a panic disorder and felt it important to do things that scare me.' Facing his fears helps him cope: when a moment of panic arises, he knows that he has conquered something even scarier.

Since March 2021, he has created more than 50 graffiti. Some are in Winchester, like the portrait of Bapsybanoo, the Indian Marchioness of Winchester, outside the Cabinet Rooms. Others are scattered across nearby towns, like the girl making a daisy chain in Bishop's Waltham or a boy on a hobby horse wearing a crown too large for his head in Salisbury.

On the brick wall in St Cross, the little boy with his kite is no longer alone. As Hendog's first public artwork began to fade, he replaced it with a slight adaptation. The boy has grown older, and a little brother sits on his shoulders, gazing skywards just like his brother once did – towards a kite that, this time, is no longer visible, yet still present.

Address *Boys with Kite*, Bridge Wall close to the Handlebar Café, Garnier Road car park, Winchester, SO23 9PA | **Getting there** A 7-minute walk from Winchester East Park & Ride | **Hours** Accessible 24 hours | **Tip** Once you have found the graffiti *Boys with Kite* head to the nearby Handlebar Café for refreshment.

10 Butler's House of Rest

Offering respite to 'recognised failures'

Five decades before women were allowed to vote, the British writer and social reformer Josephine Butler took on patriarchy without fear or hesitation. In 1870, having formed two national associations, she travelled 4,000 miles in under a year to speak at about 100 public meetings. Her objective: to overthrow the Contagious Diseases Act. This law gave police the power not only to interrogate any woman they suspected of being a prostitute but also to carry out a forcible inspection of her genitals. It was enforced at a time when many women were pressured into this profession due to a lack of basic schooling, let alone higher education, which excluded them from most career options. This was an era when women were not seen as independent individuals but as the property of their husbands – or, if unmarried, their fathers or brothers.

Nowadays, Josephine Butler's work is often associated with Liverpool, where she first became involved in helping women in need; with Oxford, where she married her husband, George; or with London, where she later lived and became the central figure in the fight against the Contagious Diseases Act. Yet one of her kindest offerings was established in Winchester.

By 1885, Josephine Butler had established a little 'house of rest' on Canon Street, at the corner of Culver Road – now known as Hamilton House and under private ownership. The house was set up as a 'faith hospital', providing shelter for girls and women deemed 'failures, morally and physically'. In her memoir, Butler writes: 'Some were sick, rejected by hospitals as incurable; others friendless, betrayed and ruined, judged for one reason or another not quite suitable for other homes or refuges.' Over time, she helped more than 40 women find solace and support in this house. And just a year after opening it, she had reason to celebrate: the Contagious Diseases Act had been repealed.

Address Hamilton House, 64 Canon Street, Winchester, SO23 9JW | **Getting there** A 16-minute walk from Winchester railway station | **Hours** Visible from the outside only | **Tip** Find out about various fascinating women who lived in the city at the Winchester City Museum.

11 The Buttercross

You shall not cross with Wintonians

In 1770, a magnificent monument caught the eye of nobleman Thomas Lee Dummer as a potential addition for his estate, Cranbury Park. This stately home near Otterbourne was once home to Sir Isaac Newton. If you ever have the opportunity to visit the grounds (the house is not generally open to the public but sometimes open days are arranged), you can find a sundial in the park, for which the astronomical calculations were made by Newton himself. It was installed by John Conduitt, who was the husband of Sir Isaac Newton's adopted daughter Catherine Barton, and who bought the estate in 1721. After Conduitt's death, house and estate were sold to the wealthy landowner Thomas Lee Dummer, and it was this landowner's son who, in 1770, wanted to leave his own mark.

Why start small, he might have thought as his eyes fell on the medieval monument in the city centre of Winchester. The multi-pinnacled cross on its tall pedestal of five octagonal steps had once been used by farmers to sell their produce: fresh and salted meat, poultry and eggs, cheese and butter. Thus, its name: Buttercross. Dummer purchased the cross from the Corporation of Winchester and, expecting swift process, sent workmen to the monument to have it disassembled. However, as author Charlotte Mary Yonge observes in her book *John Keeble's Parishes*, 'the inhabitants of the city were more conservative than their corporation'. As Dummer's workmen arrived at the Buttercross to dismantle and move it, the residents of Winchester 'made such a demonstration'.

In the end, the purchase had to be cancelled and the cross remained in its position in the High Street, where it can still be observed today. The defeated Thomas Dummer built a tall obelisk made of plaster and lath instead, which delighted the children of the estate for the next six decades until it was, as Charlotte Mary Yonge tells, destroyed by the weather.

Address Buttercross, 30 High Street, Winchester, SO23 9BL | **Getting there** A 10-minute walk from Winchester railway station | **Hours** Accessible 24 hours | **Tip** Cranbury Park, the short-term intended home for the cross, is generally not open to the public, but keep your eyes open for special public open days.

12 Cabinet Rooms

Second living room away from home

The best ideas grow on their own. When Gary and Marcus started their food blog in 2014, their initial goal was simply to shine a spotlight on culinary excellence. Soon, however, they began organising their own festivals, focusing on cocktails and gin. But then, they realised they did not just want to celebrate others' achievements, but champion this sector themselves. When the Art Café in Jewry Street was looking for a new host in 2017, the timing was perfect.

Pushing open the glass door and stepping into the comfort of the Cabinet Rooms, you immediately feel the emotional warmth. 'We wanted to create a safe space for everyone,' Gary says. A cosy second living room where people did not have to behave in a certain way but could be as wild or quiet or unconventional as they wanted. 'A little like the members of the Bloomsbury Group,' Marcus adds, referring to the 20th-century collective of artists and writers like Virginia Woolf, her sister Vanessa Bell, and artist Duncan Grant. Individuals who were 'different at a time when being different was dangerous'. To pay tribute to them, Marcus did not just hang their pictures on the wall – the entire café's design is a homage. The colours are inspired by Vanessa's portrait *Iceland Poppies* and the walls in the front room are painted in bold stripes, echoing her studio in Charleston.

Aiming to help their community flourish, the café owners also run a secret film society in the basement, offer a book club that is so popular tickets are sold out the minute they go on offer, and host an annual Men's Wellbeing Workshop. But even when you visit without an event taking place, sipping a cappuccino and eating a slice of *Hjónabandssæla* – the Icelandic happy marriage cake offering a harmonic blend of rhubarb and strawberry jam mixed with oats – it only takes a few moments for a sense of calm you did not know you needed to settle in.

Address 1–2, De Lunn Buildings, Jewry Street, Winchester, SO23 8SA | **Getting there** A 5-minute walk from Winchester railway station | **Hours** Tue 2–7pm, Wed 9am–9pm, Thu 9am–10pm, Fri & Sat 9am–11pm, Sun 10am–8pm | **Tip** Look carefully before you enter. On the outside wall, street artist Hendog has captured Bapsybanoo Pavry, Marchioness of Winchester, an Indian socialite and aristocrat.

13 Char

The finest leaves for ladies of Winchester

For a lady of refined Winchester, only the finest leaves will do: the ones from Darjeeling – the Champagne of tea, after all – mixed with bold Assam and smooth Sumatra, delicately flavoured with orange, grapefruit and bergamot. This blend, David Hazeldine advises, is for tea lovers who strive for the best. Gently, David puts the cylinder-shaped box back on the shelf.

While most people in their sixties begin thinking about retirement, David Hazeldine was only getting started. And although the shop he currently runs is deeply rooted in Winchester, its origin spans the globe. In the years after the millennium, the British entrepreneur had settled in Australia. Every morning, he would walk to a little café, but despite being a coffee lover, his attention was drawn to a shop across the road, Tea Leaves. Its arrangement, its smells and its dedication to quality fascinated him. When his son, who still lived in England, called to discuss career opportunities, David had the perfect idea.

In August 2006, father and son opened Char, a little tea boutique on Winchester High Street, selling premium leaves, working with local tea specialists in China and India to ensure the highest quality. They created a Winchester Breakfast Tea that uses mid-season Assam (which is slightly milder but, due to its richness, still ideal for the hard water of southeast England) and a Winchester Afternoon Tea, which combines strength with refinement.

In 2025, new additions arrived on the shelves. Enter Jane Austen Regency Breakfast, a fine black tea made exclusively with leaves from China (as India was not known as a tea source at the time of the great author), offering a smooth, slightly floral aroma. It evokes a time when life revolved around the fireplace and writing was done at an open window, allowing the scent of a lush English garden to drift in.

Address 156 High Street, Winchester, SO23 9BA | Getting there A short walk from Winchester bus station | Hours Mon–Sat 10am–5.30pm, Sun 11am–4pm | Tip Did you know the Winchester Hotel & Spa offers private afternoon tea parties?

14 Charlotte M Yonge's Bench

Resting with Eastleigh's name giver

When thinking of prolific Victorian authors from Hampshire, Portsmouth-born Charles Dickens might spring to mind. Or Sir Arthur Conan Doyle, who is buried in the New Forest. However, one other author should not be omitted from that list – Charlotte Mary Yonge. After all, not only did she shape a village but she also named a town in this county.

Charlotte Mary Yonge was born in 1823 in the small village of Otterbourne into a devout High Church Anglican household. Having a highly intellectual father meant that in a time when girls' education consisted of drawing, needlework and dancing, Charlotte was educated in French, Greek, Latin and algebra. Fascinated by literature and religion, she started to put pen to paper. Her novels were so well received, she became one of the most successful authors of the Victorian era, publishing more than 100 novels in her lifetime. *The Heir of Redclyffe,* which tells the spiritual and moral story of the charismatic but quick-tempered heir Guy Morville, was so popular that author J. B. Priestley claimed 'its popularity left Dickens and Thackeray well behind'.

Yonge's success allowed her to donate to various churches. In 1868, she gave the substantial sum of £500 (worth approximately £80,000 in 2025) to a new parish, which was formed just south of her home, combining the villages of Eastley and Barton. Due to her generous donation, she was asked which of the two villages the parish should be named after. Charlotte picked Eastley – but announced that she would prefer if it were spelled 'Eastleigh', as she regarded this to be more modern.

Since 2015, Eastleigh has remembered its name giver in a bronze statue outside Eastleigh railway station. Created by the artist Vivien Mallock, it depicts Charlotte sitting on a bench, reading a book – inviting the public to sit next to her to rest.

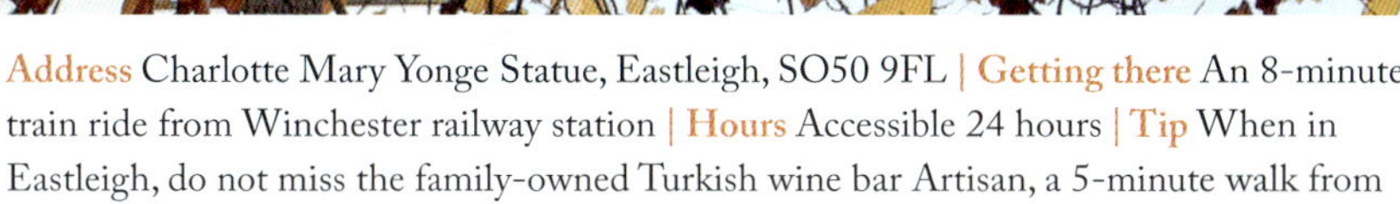

Address Charlotte Mary Yonge Statue, Eastleigh, SO50 9FL | Getting there An 8-minute train ride from Winchester railway station | Hours Accessible 24 hours | Tip When in Eastleigh, do not miss the family-owned Turkish wine bar Artisan, a 5-minute walk from Eastleigh railway station.

15 Chawton House

A Great House for women's writing

Old libraries always exude a sense of mystery, but the one at Chawton House holds a particularly empowering secret. As you walk up the gravel driveway flanked by ancient trees, it is easy to see why Jane Austen called this Elizabethan manor (situated only minutes from the cottage where she lived from 1809 to 1817) the 'Great House'.

Once a medieval hunting lodge where kings would stop, the estate was acquired by Nicholas Knight in 1578. It is the house he built – developed and shaped over centuries – that we can explore today. Marvel at the Great Hall with its impressive fireplace, and portraits of previous owners such as the formidable Elizabeth Knight (née Martin); the cosy Oak Room with its reading nook (said to have been Jane Austen's favourite spot); and the spacious Dining Room with its long wooden table, in use when Jane's brother Edward Austen Knight inherited the estate and offered the nearby cottage as a home to his mother and his two sisters.

And then, there is the Library – with a twist that might give you goosebumps. All of the 4,500 books, dating from 1660 to 1860, huddled together on tightly packed shelves, were written by women. They include rare, sometimes unique works of Aphra Behn and Frances Burney, Ann Radcliffe and Mary Wollstonecraft. In a period remembered largely through the words of men, this collection challenges the notion of what women did and were capable of in the 18th century.

The library owes its existence to an American philanthropist. By the 1990s, as the estate had fallen into disrepair and was at risk of being converted into a hotel, businesswoman Sandy Lerner stepped in. In honour of Jane Austen's legacy, she decided to create a research library and study centre focusing on women's writing. In more recent years, the manor opened its doors to a wider public, offering tours and a wide range of events, but the exhibitions on the first floor still centre on women's achievements.

Address Chawton House, Alton, Hampshire, GU34 1SJ, www.chawtonhouse.org | Getting there A 30-minute car ride from Winchester city centre; bus 64 to Alton Sports Centre, then a 25-minute walk | Hours Fri–Sun 11am–3.30pm (minimum), extended opening in summer | Tip The house offers beautiful, often Jane Austen-themed, open-air theatre productions on the grounds (see website for details).

16 Cheesefoot Head

Where Eisenhower rallied his troops

Be careful! The car park appears unexpectedly, just before the gentle peak on a racy uphill curve of the A272. Nevertheless, as you get out of your vehicle and make your way to the little gate at the bottom of the car park, you will immediately be charmed. Here, your gaze can travel far and wide: the flaxseed might gently sway in a breeze, and up in the air you may even witness the powerful dance between soaring buzzards.

Follow the little path that runs along the road until you come to another gate. If it is late spring or early summer, the air will smell citrusy fresh with elderflower, which grows in thick bunches along the South Downs path you have just entered. As you step towards the mesh fence on the other side of the trail, a wide, natural bowl opens below you. This bowl was shaped by the melting water of glaciers, which eroded the soft chalk during the last Ice Age, approximately 110,000 years ago. However, this spot wasn't just shaped by the past, it also helped shape history.

In the spring of 1944, British and American soldiers gathered in this very area to prepare for D-Day. One day, the banks filled with troops eager to witness champion Joe Louis demonstrating his skills. Later, on 6 June 1944, General Dwight D Eisenhower (then commander of the historic Operation Overlord and later the 34th President of the United States of America) shared a speech with 100,000 troops that he had been preparing for months. In it, he addressed 'Soldiers, Sailors, and Airmen of the Allied Expeditionary Force', warning them that they were 'about to embark upon the great crusade', but also inspiring optimism, by declaring that the 'tide has turned' and they would 'accept nothing less than victory'.

A recorded version of the speech was played across southern England. It is now considered one of the most listened to and most recognisable speeches in the world.

Address Cheesefoot Head, A272, Winchester, SO24 0HU | Getting there An 8-minute drive from Winchester city centre; park at Cheesefoot Head car park | Hours Accessible 24 hours | Tip The voco Winchester Hotel & Spa, only a few minutes away, offers a lovely afternoon tea as well as an indulgent spa.

17 The Chesapeake Mill

Don't give up the ship!

What could an English countryside mill and a US frigate possibly have in common? In the case of Chesapeake Mill, the answer lies at its very bones: the three-storey watermill in the idyllic village of Wickham was built using timbers salvaged from the 44-gun, three-masted, wooden-hulled frigate USS *Chesapeake*.

In late spring of 1813, Captain James Lawrence entered this ship as its new commander. He had risen to fame only four months earlier, when he sank the British warship HMS *Peacock*. Eager for another victory, he left Boston's harbour on 1 June and engaged the British HMS *Shannon* in intense battle. However, the British managed to disable their opponents in less than 12 minutes and Captain Lawrence was mortally wounded. His famous last words 'DONT [sic] GIVE UP THE SHIP' survived not only stitched on a large blue flag as ordered by his friend Oliver Hazard Perry, but also as often-repeated American naval lore.

In the meantime, the USS *Chesapeake* was transferred to English soil and, in 1819, sold in pieces by ship breaker Joshua Holmes in Portsmouth. When John Prior heard of this opportunity, he did not hesitate. Prior wanted to replace Wickham's older watermill, and the southern pine used for the deck beams was ideal. This makes Chesapeake Mill the finest example of repurposed ship timbers outside of the Royal Dockyard.

In the early 2000s, an antiquities dealer, who had marvelled at the building since he was a young boy sitting with swinging legs on the bridge opposite, seized the moment. He purchased the derelict building and in 2004, Chesapeake Mill Ltd opened as a spacious antiquity store, offering paintings and cabinets, jewellery and vintage clothes and, above all, the unique opportunity to wander beneath historic ship beams. If you look carefully, you might even detect some of the race marks and engravings of American soldiers.

Address Chesapeake Mill, Bridge Street, Wickham, Hampshire, PO17 5JH | **Getting there** Take 69 bus to The Square, Wickham | **Hours** Landmark visible 24 hours; Antiquity store open Tue–Sat 10am–5pm, Sun 11am–4pm | **Tip** Visit nearby Woodies, a tearoom and bistro, for eggs benedict, sweet waffles or classic cod and chips.

18 The Chesil Rectory

Dining in medieval charm

'Oh,' Eleanor Dodd says as her gaze travels across the small rooms, 'if these walls could talk.' The iconic Chesil Rectory, with its two symmetrical gables, sturdy timber beams and the warm glow spilling from its casement windows, is not only one of Winchester's most recognisable historical buildings, but also the oldest commercial building still in use. As you take the steps down to the ancient wooden entrance with its narrow front door (once used by livestock), you are struck by its remarkable age. The name nods to its long history, too. 'Chesil' derives from the Old English word 'ceosel' or 'cisel' referring to a bank of gravel or shingle. In the past, the River Itchen would have been much wider, with the house gables sitting right on its bank.

Originally built by a merchant between 1425 and 1450, it has been an antiques shop, a tannery, a shoemaker, Winchester's first Sunday School, and a tearoom – until it found its current calling as one of the city's most atmospheric dining venues.

Eleanor and Mark Dodd had originally been looking for a little bar to open in Winchester, but when the old Chesil Rectory came onto the market in 2008 they jumped at the opportunity. At a time when fine dining was still more associated with French cuisine, the couple, together with head chef Damian Brown, wanted to showcase the bounty of local produce on Hampshire's doorstep in an elegant dining experience: crisp, honey-glazed duck, buttery south coast cod served with sun-ripened tomatoes from the Isle of Wight, and peppery, slightly tingling watercress from Alresford.

Seated on soft velvet chairs underneath honey-coloured silk lampshades, you feel enveloped by the soothing dark walls and heavy curtains, intrigued by the French chandeliers and botanical prints. Today, as well as offering an à la carte menu, The Chesil Rectory also hosts quarterly wine tastings, welcoming producers and winemakers from all over the world.

Address The Chesil Rectory, 1 Chesil Street, Winchester, SO23 0HU | Getting there A 4-minute walk from Winchester bus station | Hours Mon–Fri noon–3.30pm & 5.30–11pm, Sat noon–3.30pm & 6–11pm, Sun noon–4pm & 6–10pm | Tip Before or after your lunch, why not stroll along the beautiful River Itchen?

19 Chesil Theatre

The magic of a community stage

It was a bright day in the late 1980s: Paul Riddell remembers it clearly. New to Winchester and in search of a theatre company, he paused at the red door of a little church, left slightly ajar. Through the pointed medieval gate, he glimpsed people on tall ladders, arranging lights and props on a little stage for what was about to become the set of a new play. Curious, Paul stepped inside – and the warm welcome he received moved him so much he didn't think twice about auditioning for the theatre's next play, Dario Fo's *Can't Pay? Won't Pay!* Nearly four decades later, he has not only appeared in dozens of performances, but he has also become chairman of Winchester's leading amateur theatre.

Founded in 1863, Winchester's Dramatic Society made its home in the medieval St Peter's Church on Chesil Street in 1966. Known now as Chesil Theatre, the venue stages eight or nine productions a year in its intimate studio-style auditorium. The productions transport audiences from the lightness of *Shakespeare in Love* to the life of Ruth Ellis – the last woman hanged in Britain – in *The Thrill of Love* or a clash with some *Nasty Neighbours*.

The theatre's mission extends beyond entertainment; it seeks to nurture – holding open auditions, offering weekly youth drama workshops and inviting playwrights every other year to participate in its TakeTen festival.

Soon, the society will be able to offer an even better experience. By 2028, Chesil Theatre plans to modernise its historic home through a £2.1 million development project and appeal. A new extension will make the theatre more comfortable and accessible for the audience, improve safety and flexibility for the performers and secure its legacy. For the power of theatre, Paul knows, extends beyond the magic of a successful evening: it can help to overcome speech impediments, forge lasting friendships and uncover a confidence you never knew you had.

Address Chesil Theatre, Chesil Street, Winchester, SO23 0HU | Getting there A 5-minute walk from Winchester bus station | Hours Open to ticketholders only | Tip Before your show, treat yourself to dinner at Kyoto Kitchen, just one minute's walk from the theatre.

20 Cheyney Court

The onlooker's favourite

Chances are, when you reach this lovely old timbered house – with its overhanging frame resting atop a sturdy stone base, its three charming gables huddled close together and the magnificent wisteria generously gushing soft violet and fresh green hues across the arch on the side – you will find people standing in front of it, smartphones or cameras raised. Cheyney Court, nestled against the old city walls and the elegant Priory Gate (which is topped by a tiny room) is possibly the most photographed domestic building in the city. But what is its use? And where does its name stem from?

In medieval England, the law was enforced not only by the monarch but also by the Church. Consequently, ecclesiastical courts were established – run by bishops and governed by canon law, the law of the Church. Cheyney Court serves as an example of such a bishop's courthouse. As for its name, when looking through the list of former churchmen of Winchester, a name immediately attracts attention: from 1744 to 1748, the Anglican priest Thomas Cheyney served as Dean of Winchester. His father, also named Thomas Cheyney, had been a master at Winchester College. However, Thomas was never bishop, and the building existed long before his tenure – it was erected in 1479. Thus, he seems an unlikely namesake. However, there is another explanation: 'The name Cheyney', writes Telford Varley, historian and first headmaster of Peter Symonds School, in his book *Winchester* in June 1910, 'appears to be derived from the French *chêne*, an oak. The term could have referred to the "oak beneath the shadow of which it was originally held", its ordinary sessions being fixed for the Thursday in each week.'

In the 19th century, the court became a residential building, the hall giving way to living spaces and bedrooms. While it has been used to house the head teachers at nearby Pilgrims' School, in January 2025 the house returned to the market, to be let at £7,000 per month.

Address Cheyney Court, The Close, Winchester, SO23 9LS | Getting there A 17-minute walk from Winchester railway station | Hours Accessible 24 hours | Tip There is another intriguing example of a courthouse in Hampshire: the Court House of East Meon, a 30-minute car ride east of Winchester.

21 Chocolate Craft

The fillings of sweet delight

'Oh, wow!' As Pippa Sherry presents the delicate little chocolates – some topped with tiny pieces of orange or freeze-dried raspberry, one even adorned with a finely shaped crescent moon – a murmur of disbelief travels around the room. But Pippa leaves no space for self-doubt – just as you might expect from a former nurse. Instead, she plunges straight into action: passing samples of dark, milk, white and the surreally pink ruby chocolate around the room, offering just the right amount of information to convey which essences and ingredients pair best in a ganache. Then she supervises as the group cautiously starts to fill the moulds with combinations like dark chocolate and ginger, or white chocolate mixed with Marc de Champagne.

In the chilled surroundings of a converted farmhouse in Old Alresford, Pippa Sherry runs Chocolate Craft, a small chocolate factory producing hand-crafted truffles and confectionery – in their busiest months as many as 60,000 of them. Chocolate Craft supplies not only regional florists and hotels but also national treasures: in 2024, their hand-piped plaques even made it into Fortnum & Mason's Paddington Bear Hamper, with all 600 pieces selling out in just three hours.

Pippa came to the chocolate factory – or really the previous owner came to her – after she had been working as a nurse for 30 years and was looking for a career change. She first found herself decorating plates when the former owner of Chocolate Craft asked if she would like to join. 'Artists are the best chocolatiers,' she says.

A good two hours after the group was first shown the model chocolates, it is time to take their own creations out of the fridge. This time, gasps of surprise ripple around the room: the little drops of milk on white chocolate have, indeed, settled into perfect crescent moons.

Address Chocolate Craft, Unit 1, Upton Park Farm, Old Alresford, Hampshire, SO24 9EB, www.chocolatecraft.co.uk | Getting there Bus 64 to Broad Street, New Alresford, then a 23-minute walk | Hours By prior arrangement only | Tip Curious about trying one of Pippa's creations? You can also buy the chocolate treats at the little eatery Mange 2 on Alresford High Street.

22 The City Mill

Turner-ing to nature

During the Georgian era, as many as 20,000 watermills existed across Britain, yet only a fraction of these have survived to the present day. One of the oldest is Winchester's City Mill, whose earliest records estimate its origin at A. D. 932. This makes it only one year younger than the world's oldest example, Priston Mill near Bath, Somerset. Whilst most watermills are located far from urban areas, this one can be found in the very heart of the city.

Over the centuries, Winchester City Mill's production level has been ebbing and flowing with the times. In 1086, for example, the mill was among the country's most productive mills, but due to climate change, the plague and economic hardship, was listed as derelict in 1471. In 1554, Queen Mary gifted the mill to the city as part of her wedding settlement. Yet, given its state, it is questionable how well received this gift was. Two hundred years later, new hope arrived in the form of tanner James Cooke, who rebuilt the mill. But by 1828, it was again threatened with demolition and turned into a hostel. Finally, in 2004, after diligent restoration, the grindstones turned once more, 90 years after they had last worked.

In 2013, a minor frenzy erupted when the mill's assistant manager browsed the recently digitalised archive of Tate Modern and discovered a sketch by J. M. W. Turner depicting this very mill. Turner had toured the Isle of Wight in 1795 when he was a 20-year-old student at the Royal Academy, and in the course of his field trip also visited Winchester. Apart from the giant West Window of Winchester Cathedral, he also painted the mill, immediately recognisable by its pointed roof, brick arches and distinctive window position. A print of the original sketch is displayed inside the mill, which also houses a small island garden as a surreal wildlife spot in the middle of the city.

Address Winchester City Mill, Bridge Street, Winchester, SO23 0EJ | Getting there A short walk from Winchester bus station | Hours Landmark visible 24 hours; watermill & cafe open Thu–Sun 10am–4pm, closed Christmas & Boxing Day | Tip There is an absolute culinary must-visit a few doors down: Kyoto Kitchen serves fantastic Japanese cuisine.

23 The Crown Inn

Housing the enemy

It is, undeniably, in the nature of an inn to host guests. But it may come as a surprise that the historic pub situated in The Square in Bishop's Waltham once accommodated the very admiral who commanded the French fleet against the English at the Battle of Trafalgar – albeit not entirely of his own choosing.

During the Napoleonic Wars, thousands of French – and some Spanish – officers were taken as prisoners of war. While medieval castles such as Portchester or Edinburgh were repurposed as prisoner-of-war depots, the British also designated more than 60 'parole towns' – one of them was quaint Bishop's Waltham. In these towns, 200 to 300 officers would settle in rural country or market settings, sometimes for several years. It must have been a surreal experience, in a time of conflict and long before international travel, for the British and French communities to share social spaces.

Whilst most officers were accommodated in houses around the town, some stayed at The Crown Inn, a charming timber-framed, 16th-century coaching inn, once famous for cockfighting and now offering British classics and delicate rooms with finely carved wooden furniture. The most famous French resident – alongside Ambroise-Louis Garneray, who painted some of his sea scenes from memory – was Pierre-Charles-Jean-Baptiste-Silvestre de Villeneuve, the admiral who ordered the French fleet to break out of Cádiz, Spain, thereby triggering Nelson's famous tactic of dividing his fleet into two columns in order to break the enemy's line.

After hours of fierce battling, in which around 8,500 men were killed, Villeneuve surrendered and was eventually moved to Bishop's Waltham. He was repatriated in 1806 but died later that year of seven stab wounds to the chest. Though officially recorded as a suicide, speculation has persisted: did Napoleon seek revenge for the failed battle?

Address The Crown Inn, The Square, Bishop's Waltham, SO32 1AF | **Getting there** Take bus 69 to Winchester, alight at The Square | **Hours** Mon–Sat, 9am–11pm, Sun 9am–10pm | **Tip** To work up an appetite, follow the 3-mile Bishop's Waltham Nature Walk. You can find directions at www.hants.gov.uk.

24 Design Junction

Art for all

One moment, the clay sits like an off-white pudding with blue dots on a round plate. But as Amy presses the foot pedal, the wheel begins to spin. The ceramic artist then seems to press only lightly into the centre with calm precision before pulling smoothly along the sides and the unformed chunk transforms into a slender blue and white marbled bowl. It is oddly satisfying to watch a skilful potter help clay take shape.

Although your first bowl will likely look far less elegant (unless, of course, you are about to discover a hidden talent), it is even more relaxing to give it a try yourself. In an ever-accelerating world, it does wonders to one's mental health to take a break and spin a clay wheel – not to make a perfect teacup, but to have three hours focusing entirely on what is right in front of you. Because if your mind wanders, your clay will, too.

When Jakob Davies and Amy Murphy met at university, they soon discovered a shared desire to create a space not only to master their own craft but to help others flourish as well. In 2018, Jake, a painter, began offering life drawing lessons in various places around Winchester. Then luck offered them the very venue he'd had an eye on for years. Within six months, they had transformed the two-storey workshop, painting the rooms in calming colours, adding worktops and shelves to display their creations.

In November 2022, they opened their art studio Design Junction, offering throwing workshops, pottery painting, tufting and crafts sessions. Since then, the studio has grown to a team of eight and Jake has learnt that art has no age limit: participants have been as young as 11 (attending with parents) to as old as 91. Amid the hustle and bustle of running a business, he still finds time to work with clay almost daily, so that maybe, one day, his designs will be as refined as Amy's.

Address Design Junction, 5–6 Kings Walk, Winchester, SO23 8AF, www.designjunctionwinchester.co.uk | Getting there A 4-minute walk from Winchester bus station | Hours Mon–Sat 11am–2pm, Sun 11am–3pm; see website for details of workshops | Tip This corner of Winchester is a crafty one. Just a couple of metres down, Bella Craft offers lovely workshops, too.

25 The Eclipse Inn

Venturing into the room in red

If you step inside the beautiful black-and-white Tudor house at number 25 The Square – now the Eclipse Inn – you will likely hear tales of hauntings said to occur within its walls: curious light orbs caught on video, scratchy sounds from above and an old woman whom guests claim to have spoken to upstairs when nobody was supposed to be there. You might then venture up to the first floor. Climbing the wonky staircase and ducking beneath a low doorframe, you arrive in a room so crimson it takes your breath away. But given what is said to have happened in this room, the colour could not be more appropriate.

On 1 September 1685, the 71-year-old Dame Alice Lisle was escorted into this room, before the guards bolted the door. Did she get even a minute's sleep? Did she try to suppress the clinking and thumping echoing through the window?

Born into a wealthy Hampshire family, Alice married the lawyer and parliamentarian John Lisle at the age of 19. When the English monarchy was restored in 1660, he worried for his safety and fled to Switzerland (where he was eventually assassinated). Alice, however, remained in England and continued to sympathise with the Nonconformists opposed to the crown. In July 1685, she gave shelter at her home, Moyles Court, to the Nonconformist minister John Hickes and Richard Nelthorpe, a lawyer convicted of lawlessness. For that, Alice Lisle was arrested for treason.

After spending the night in the red room, Alice stepped through the window onto a scaffolding hastily erected in the square below. Initially, the infamous Judge Jeffreys had sentenced her to be burned at the stake, but King James II intervened and commuted the sentence to beheading – a form of execution seen as more befitting her social status. Alice Lisle was the last woman to be publicly beheaded in England, and her trial is now widely considered a miscarriage of justice.

Address The Eclipse Inn, 25 The Square, Winchester, SO23 9EX | Getting there A 12-minute walk from Winchester railway station | Hours Daily Sun–Thu 11am–11pm, Fri & Sat 11am–1am | Tip If you enjoy haunted stories of the past, you might be interested in the Winchester Ghost Walk.

26 Farley Mount Monument

Never forget: Beware Chalk Pit

The white obelisk, with its little red gables on three sides, peeking into the afternoon sky, could be mistaken for a religious building. Positioned on a little mount isolated in a field, you might assume it to be the burial ground of a former lord or leader. Neither is true. Step into the opening of Farley Mount Monument, and a stone plaque informs you about its true purpose: *Underneath lies buried a horse* the inscription begins, and ends with the phrase *in the name of "Beware Chalk Pit"*.

The horse with this unusual name once belonged to Sir Paulet St John, son of the manor at Farley Chamberlayne. Appointed High Sheriff of Hampshire at the age of 23, he later became a politician in the House of Commons and, in his late sixties, Mayor of Winchester. In September 1733, aged 29, the avid horseman was out foxhunting, when his horse leapt into a chalk pit nearly eight metres deep. As if by miracle, both horse and rider survived the incident unscathed. Only weeks later, Sir Paulet St John entered a race at Winchester's Worthy Downs with this very horse – and won the Hunters' Plate. Legend has it, Sir Paulet credited the victory to the horse's new name: 'Beware Chalk Pit'.

So devoted was the politician to his favourite animal that – after its death – he commissioned a monument that has stood ever since as a curious but cherished landmark.

In order to visit it, park at the Farley Mount car park (or, if you want a longer walk, at Crab Wood car park at the entrance of the country park). From Farley Mount car park, follow Clarendon Way uphill. At a fork in the road, turn left and continue climbing. The sharp, white peak will soon come into view. Sitting 174 metres above sea level, the mount offers an impressive view of the soft rolling fields stretching as far as Hursley and Braishfield, and looks particularly beautiful during a spring sunset.

Address Hampshire Farley, Mount Road, Winchester, SO51 0QT | **Getting there** A 10-minute walk from Farley Mount car park on Farley Mount Road, Winchester, SO21 2JG | **Hours** Accessible 24 hours | **Tip** Feeling hungry after the walk? Stop at the cosy four-star hotel and restaurant The King's Head in Hursley, only a 10-minute drive away.

27 Florence Nightingale Memorial

Remembering the Lady of the Lamp

Florence Nightingale is mostly associated with London, where she spent much of her life; with the Italian city Florence, where she was born in 1820 and after which she was named; and with Crimea, where she became famous as the 'Lady of the Lamp' as for her devoted care of wounded soldiers and her work to improve sanitation during the Crimean War. Yet the world's most famous nurse's final resting place can be found just a short drive away from Winchester.

In 1826, after the Nightingale family had returned from Italy to England, Florence's father William Nightingale purchased Embley Park, a stately home, as their new family home (it now houses an independent school). It was at Embley Park that Florence Nightingale claims she received her divine call. 'God spoke to me and called me to His Service,' she wrote in February 1837, aged 16. 'What form this service was to take the voice did not say.' That same year, she gained her first experience of nursing during an influenza outbreak at Embley.

In 1862, after her groundbreaking work during the Crimean War and meetings with Queen Victoria, a professional assignment brought her back to Hampshire. She was asked to advise on the design of the new Royal Hampshire County Hospital in Winchester. Her suggestions, such as well-lit wards, ventilated rooms and the separation of patients with venereal diseases, were all accepted.

When Florence Nightingale died in London aged 90, her family was offered a burial in Westminster Abbey. However, they declined and chose to bury her alongside her parents at the family memorial instead. Thus, her body was carried to Hampshire, brought by train to Romsey and then taken to East Wellow. You can find her memorial at St Margaret of Antioch's Church, where it stands out between weathered gravestones, built from stone as bright as the light of her lamp.

Address Grave of Florence Nightingale, St Margaret of Antioch's Church, Hackleys Lane, West Wellow, Romsey, SO51 6DR | Getting there A 26-minute car ride from Winchester centre | Hours Accessible 24 hours | Tip Combine the visit with a stop at the cute Headlands Farm Coffee Shop nearby (www.headlandsfarm.co.uk).

28 Gilbert White's House

Meet the willow warbler, harvest mouse and noctule bat

You probably know that the Bible is the most popular book in the English language. You might also be aware that Shakespeare is the second most quoted English author. But did you know that the fourth most published book in this language was created in the southeast corner of Hampshire?

In the endearing village of Selborne, a wrought-iron gate welcomes you to Gilbert White's House and Garden. Born in 1720, Gilbert White was a clergyman – but beyond studying scriptures for his sermons, he also loved to observe the natural world. With great patience, he studied the flowering times of plants, the migration routine of birds and even the hibernation pattern of his pet tortoise Timothy. He was the first to identify the willow warbler, the chiffchaff and the wood warbler as distinct species; he also pioneered descriptions of the noctule bat and the harvest mouse. In 1789, he published his groundbreaking work *The Natural History of Selborne*, a book that explains his work and findings in charming letters and that has earned him the title 'the father of ecology'.

A visit to his former home allows you to peek into his bedroom, complete with the four-poster bed draped in delicate floral embroidery. Further along, you find his slightly untidy study – a scene that recalls Gilbert's own description of the room 'where tattered volumes / strew the learned ground, Where Novels – Sermons, in confusion lie / Law, ethics, physics, school-divinity'. Displays show the species he helped to distinguish. And then, back on the ground floor, you encounter the true treasure. The original manuscript of *The Natural History of Selborne*. The handwriting is impeccably neat and fills each page from edge to edge – a fitting hallmark for a careful observer like Gilbert and wholly appropriate for a book that has remained in print for nearly a quarter of a millennium.

'Your work …
will immortalize your Place of Abode
as well as Yourself.'

Address The Wakes, High Street, Selborne, Alton, GU34 3JH, www.gilbertwhiteshouse.org.uk | Getting there Take bus 64 to Alton Railway station and bus 38 to The Selbourne Arms, then a short walk | Hours 21 Jul–30 Aug daily 10.30am–4.30pm; 1 Apr–20 Jul & 1 Sep–31 Oct, Tue–Sun 10.30am–4.30pm; 1 Nov–21 Dec & 2 Jan–31 Mar, Tue–Sun 10.30am–4pm | Tip The village of Selborne is the ideal starting point for exploring the natural world – for example, by following the 21-mile-long Hangers Way.

29 The Grange at Northington

Revival of the Greeks

Infinite shades of green stretch either side of the country road, when, all of a sudden, the house comes into view. Still some distance away, the Doric columns are clearly visible, and the sharp edges of the portico cut into the blue sky. It is hard to imagine that the Grange of Northington, one of the grandest examples of neoclassical residences in the Greek Revival style, was nearly demolished half a century ago.

To trace its story, we must go back to 1662, when lawyer and politician Sir Robert Henley bought the estate known as The Grange. A few years later, he commissioned architect William Samwell to build a more impressive house, and Samwell delivered a grand brick residence. The staircase was particularly magnificent and led writer Horace Walpole to describe the interiors as 'beautiful models of the purest and most-classic antiquity'. Over a century later, the mansion was acquired by banker Henry Drummond, whose grandson, also named Henry – affluent and impulsive – desired something grander. He commissioned architect William Wilkins, who would later design the National Gallery in London, to transform the house into a colossal Greek temple. Wilkins added a Doric portico, emulating the Theseion in Athens, and imposing side elevations.

However, once the project was finished, Drummond lost interest – and sold the residence to his neighbour, the financier Alexander Baring. But as the Baring family fortune dwindled, the estate fell into disrepair. In 1972, John Baring, 7th Lord Ashburton, organised an auction 'to strip the house of all its saleable fittings' – including the doors, marble cladding and even the grand staircase. John Baring then announced his intention to demolish the building. Yet, thanks to an outcry in *The Times*, this would be prevented – a festival was launched and in 2009 even the restored staircase could resume its intended function.

Address Northington Road, Alresford, SO24 9TG | Getting there Take the Velvet Bus 67 to Itchen Abbas or Mervyns Coaches 95, 96 to Lunways Inn, then a 3-mile walk | Hours The grounds are open most days throughout the year (see www.english-heritage.org.uk for details) | Tip For refreshments after your explorations, head to nearby New Alresford. The Club Sandwich at The Swan Hotel is particularly recommended.

30 The Grave of Thomas Thetcher

When hot, drink strong or none at all

Among the few weathered gravestones remaining in the grounds of Winchester Cathedral, one stands out for its international importance. Walking from Minster Lane to the cathedral, you can easily spot a large, grey slab filled with a long inscription. The gravestone (or to be correct, an earlier version, as the current one is a replacement from 1966) was erected by a group of Hampshire grenadiers, who were saddened by the sudden death of one of their friends. Thomas Thetcher was only 26 years old when he died on a hot 12th of May in 1764 after drinking a small beer and catching a violent fever, from which he never recovered.

In 1918, this gravestone caught the attention of American soldier Bill Wilson, on his way to the Western Front. Maybe Bill was moved by the fate of a fellow soldier; maybe the name stuck with him because it was close to that of his friend, Ebby Thacher.

Bill survived the Great War but back in America he did not find peace. He started to drink. He drank so much that he never completed law school. He drank so much that he couldn't run his business. In 1933, he was admitted to Towns Hospital and told he would either die of alcoholism or end up in an asylum. During his fourth stay at the hospital, he had a religious awakening – and never touched a drink again.

In the hope that he might inspire others, he recorded his journey in writing. Starting with a moment he had not forgotten: 'I visited Winchester Cathedral. Much moved, I wandered outside. My attention was caught by a doggerel on an old tombstone: *Here lies a Hampshire Grenadier / Who caught his death / Drinking cold small beer / A good soldier is ne'er forgot / Whether he dieth by musket / Or by pot.*' The movement Bill started became Alcoholics Anonymous. And the 'Big Book', which aims to help its followers and is one of the best-selling books of all time, still begins with this anecdote.

Address Winchester Cathedral, 9 The Close, Winchester, SO23 9LS | **Getting there** A 13-minute walk from Winchester railway station | **Hours** Accessible 24 hours | **Tip** You can find the original gravestone safely stored in a corridor at Hampshire's Regimental Museum (kindly ask the porter and they will show you).

31 The Great Hall

King Arthur's Round Table

Edward I was not only an admirer of Arthurian legends, he was also determined to connect himself to the legendary 'Once and Future King'. During his visit to Glastonbury with Queen Eleanor in 1278, Edward demanded the tomb, which was believed to hold the remains of King Arthur and Queen Guinevere, be opened so he could rebury them. (It is said that the bones of the king and queen were found in two separate chests along with their portraits and arms.) In 1283, after defeating the Welsh Prince Llewellyn, Edward claimed to have recovered King Arthur's crown. (It was allegedly presented to Westminster Abbey and disappeared afterwards, although some doubt it ever existed.) Edward's fascination with the Arthurian myth did not end there. He also commissioned the construction of a massive wooden table, 18 feet in diameter and weighing more than a ton. It is believed he paraded this Round Table during his first Arthurian tournament, held near Winchester in 1290.

Centuries later, Edward's descendant King Henry VIII went one step further and connected himself with the legendary hero. Reviving the table from neglect, he had it repainted and ensured that Arthur's portrait was rendered to his own image. Today, it hangs on the west wall of the Great Hall – one of the finest surviving aisled halls from medieval times. The hall was part of Winchester Castle, which was built in 1067, one of the most important fortresses in England and the centre of the country's administrative offices until the seat of power moved to London.

In the end, the kings' efforts to link themselves to Arthurian legend may have helped to anchor the myth in Hampshire. When the medieval author Thomas Malory wrote *Le Morte d'Arthur* in 1470, he identified Winchester as Camelot. In his account, the sword of knight Sir Balin floats 'down the stream to the City of Camelot, that is in English Winchester'.

Address Castle Avenue, SO23 8UJ, www.historicwinchester.co.uk | Getting there A 7-minute walk from Winchester railway station | Hours Daily 10am–5pm but check in advance for private events | Tip Don't miss the chance to explore Queen Eleanor's tranquil garden at the back of the Great Hall.

32 The Guildhall

Find the painting hidden under Charles I

Strolling down Winchester High Street and reaching the end as it turns into The Broadway, your gaze will undoubtedly fall on the spectacular brick building, its turrets and arches conveying nothing less than parliamentary esteem. On 22 December 1871, Viscount Eversley, the second-longest-serving Speaker of the House of Commons, laid the foundation stone for the New Guildhall. It replaced the earlier guildhall further up the road and stands on the site of St Mary's Abbey. Less than two years later, on 18 May 1873, the first Earl of Selborne and then Lord Chancellor of Britain, officially opened it.

For many years, the grand Victorian building in the heart of Winchester exhibited local artworks. These days, its impressive rooms function as event venues, offering candlelight concerts, country roadshows or pre-Christmas highlights like the Festive Fizz, where fantastic local vineyards like Black Chalk, Exton Park and Hambledon offer complimentary tastings (included in the ticket).

If you ever have the chance to attend an event or function in the King Charles Hall, take a closer look at the portrait of King Charles I. In 2017, as part of a restoration project, the portrait was sent to The Brick House (specialists in fine art conservation) in the hope of confirming the well-known court painter Peter Lely as its creator. Yet something far more significant emerged. First, conservators discovered that the sceptre in Charles' hand had originally been a staff, which was later painted over. Then, they realised that the king's head was not painted by the same hand as the rest of the body. Indeed, the head really was not to Lely's standards. Finally, an inscription was found, linking the work to Henry Jermyn, Earl of St Albans. These clues led to a striking conclusion: the painting, an original by Lely, had later been overpainted with King Charles' head.

Address Winchester Guildhall, The Broadway, Winchester, SO23 9GH, www.guildhallwinchester.co.uk | Getting there A short walk from Winchester railway station | Hours Tickets required for events (see website for details) | Tip Fancy creating your own art? Art-K offers brilliant Sip & Paint art classes in Winchester (www.adult.art-k.co.uk).

33_Gurkha Museum

Where courage crosses continents

When the British East India Company fought the Kingdom of Nepal during the Anglo-Nepalese War, the British couldn't help but be impressed by their enemy's soldiers – their toughness, skill and bravery. Even in defeat, the Gurkhas' spirit impressed their adversaries so deeply that peace in 1816 came with an unusual decision: to enlist them as allies rather than face them again as enemies. Since then, the Gurkhas have fought alongside the British soldiers in nearly every major conflict: they played a crucial role in suppressing the Indian Rebellion of 1857; more than 90,000 Gurkhas fought with the British during World War I and 130,000 Gurkhas served during World War II.

When four regiments joined the British Army and moved to Church Crookham, Hampshire, in the late 1940s, officers and veterans started to collect memorabilia. In 1974, the collection of medals, diaries, *khukuri* knives and uniforms had grown so large that Field Marshal Lord Harding opened the first museum dedicated to the elite force. Soon, it became apparent that more space was needed. When the Peninsula Barracks in Winchester ceased to be used as a training depot, the ideal spot was found.

These days, the Winchester Barracks hold the only Gurkha Museum outside of Nepal. Strolling through the Short Barrack Block, you can meet extraordinary figures like Rifleman Kulbir Thapa, who became the first Gurkha to receive the Victoria Cross, for rescuing three wounded soldiers from No Man's Land in 1915 – one of the 10 Victoria Crosses entrusted to the museum. You can learn about Lieutenant-Colonel John Manners-Smith, who received the VC after capturing a steeply defended position in today's Pakistan. And finally, you can study the portraits of Captain Michael Allmand and Rifleman Tul Bahadur Pun, who fought bravely to capture the city of Mogaung – the son of a London University professor and a soldier from a remote Nepalese village, united in a common cause.

Address The Gurkha Museum, Peninsula Barracks, Romsey Road, Winchester, SO23 8TS | Getting there A 10-minute walk from Winchester railway station | Hours Mon–Sat 10am–5pm | Tip For a deeper taste of Nepalese culture, visit the Gurkha's Inn on City Road.

34 Hampshire Hog

The animal to rule the county

David Kemp has a tendency to work with unusual materials. The British artist – born in London, raised in Canada, trained in Farnham and at Wimbledon School of Art, and now based in Cornwall – has sculpted huge, imposing Transformers out of discarded materials from old industrial sites, humorous dragons out of disused farm machinery and a pack of dogs made from miners' boots. 'I like the duality of it,' the artist explains. He sees his work as a comment, a reaction. 'Sometimes, I would even pretend I am an archaeologist from the future, reconstructing the machines and exhibiting the remains of a distant past.'

Nevertheless, in the late 1980s, Hampshire County Council commissioned him to work with a more traditional medium: to mark the institution's centenary, David Kemp was commissioned to depict the county's most famous animal.

For centuries, wild boars freely foraged through the thick forests of Hampshire. Hunters found in them challenging targets and royal parties would regularly ascend onto these fields. Indeed, King William II, William Rufus, met his death while out hunting in the New Forest. Over time, the boar was domesticated and gave rise to the Hampshire Hog, a breed known for its meat quality, robust nature and distinctive black-and-white band across the body. In the 18th century, the phrase turned into a nickname for the locals, initially possibly referring to their agricultural background, later turning into a term of endearment. In true local fashion, the H is often dropped, typical for the regional accent.

In 1898, David Kemp's bronze statue of the Hampshire Hog was officially unveiled and has been guarding the entrance to the council ever since. Despite being cast from traditional material, the statue holds special value for the artist: it was the work that paid his way through art school.

Address The Hampshire Hog, Winchester, SO23 8BH | Getting there A 6-minute walk from Winchester railway station | Hours Accessible 24 hours | Tip Only a couple of steps from the sculpture, you can find the impressive Winchester Plague Museum, which commemorates those who died during the plague in 1666.

35 Hampshire Pantry

Fall in love with fresh farming produce

It all started with the chutney. A savoury spread served with dishes at the Shoe Inn in Exton, it proved so popular customers wanted to take it home. So, the owners decided to offer exactly that. The little jars of homemade chutney were so sought after, the idea of something bigger took shape – a place filled with quality produce for people's kitchens. On 5 August 2024, the doors of the Hampshire Pantry opened for the first time.

Set in a farm barn just a few minutes outside of Winchester, the collective, combined with two local Winchester farmers, now run the Pantry, a farm shop offering not only their famous chutney but meats, cheese and home-grown vegetables from their regenerative, beyond organic market garden. Alongside sit the Blue Hour Coffee Roastery, OG artisanal gelateria using Hampshire milk, the little Pot Shop selling antiques, and a café serving pastries, homemade cakes, coffee roasted from across the courtyard, as well as a seasonal, produce-led menu.

Approaching from the car park, gravel crunching underfoot, you are immediately drawn to the open view stretching to your right, past the little outdoor seating area, with its dainty sage-green furniture. Inside the barn, large, sturdy tables sit beneath a high ceiling, strung with fairy lights; an intriguing contrast in a city known for its comfortable but compact spaces.

'We've turned into a little bit of a local escape, especially on days when the city feels very packed,' assistant manager Emily Millen explains, though within its first 18 months, the Hampshire Pantry itself got quite busy, too. 'During our pick-your-own pumpkin weekends, we had queues snaking all the way up back to the car park.' Yet, with the soothing view and the promise of a smooth coffee together with delicious scrambled eggs on toast, this is a queue you are quite happy to join.

Address Hampshire Pantry, Badger Farm Road, SO23 9RZ | Getting there Take bus 1 to Bushfield Roundabout, then a 12-minute walk | Hours Daily 8am–5pm | Tip Complete your visit with a walk around the rolling hills; use the AllTrails app for different options.

36 Hampshire Soap Company

Dreams of cedarwood

'Which fragrance is your favourite?' Maybe the warm, woody cedarwood mixed with herbaceous lavender and citrusy sweet orange? Debra Valvona Johnson nods, picks up the respective amber glass bottles and instructs you to add a few droplets of each into a tiny measuring cup. Behind her, soft morning sunshine spills through the studio window. On a solid wooden shelf, dozens of differently coloured soaps are stacked in neat packages; among them are soap boxes with well-known names: Jane Austen and Winchester Cathedral.

As with many successful businesses, this project was born out of necessity. When Debra's children were still young, two of them developed eczema, which kept them from sleeping. When Debra was trying to find a natural product that would help to ease their inflammation, she came across a soap made of goat's milk and oats. 'And it was fabulous,' she says, eyes sparkling. So inspired was Debra about this product, she quickly wondered whether she might not be able to make these herself.

When she mixed oils and essences for the first time, she would never have anticipated the outcome. These days, she not only provides soaps for the gift shop of Winchester Cathedral and Sir Harold Hillier Gardens, creating up to 300 bars of soap a day; in the private studio at the edge of her property, she also introduces others to the art of soap making.

Time for the soap magic: saponification. Equipped with safety goggles and gloves, Debra adds sodium hydroxide to the bowl. Then she takes a handheld mixer and, although she has said that the process will be instantaneous, it is astonishing to see how quickly the liquid turns solid. Minutes later, the soap is filled into its forms, dried rose petals sprinkled on top and the scent of cedarwood, lavender and sweet orange fills the air. It is so enticing that it will be hard to wait the six weeks for the soap to cure before it can be used.

Address Hampshire Soap Company, Chandlers Ford, SO53 3HD, www.hampshiresoap.com | **Getting there** Take bus 1 to Leigh Road, then a short walk | **Hours** Advance booking required (see website for details) | **Tip** You can buy the soap in many places, including the cute little West Lea Farmshop in Alresford.

37 Hartley Mauditt

The long-forgotten village

On a narrow country lane, just south of Worldham between Alton and Bordon, you pass a peaceful pond to your left and a little church to your right. So inconspicuous is St Leonard's Church, you might not give it a second glance. Alas, you should! This 900-year-old building is the only structure that remains of the 'deserted medieval village' (as it is described in the Ordnance Survey maps) of Hartley Mauditt.

Its name hints at its story. The word 'Hartley', found in a number of Hampshire villages, is probably of Saxon origin, and refers to a woodland clearing. As people began to travel, they needed to add a second name to differentiate the Hartleys. In this case, the name was taken from the nearby manor. According to the Domesday Book, William Mauditt was granted a manor at this site in 1086. At the time, the household consisted of eight villagers as well as five smallholders, and had eight ploughlands, six acres of meadow, and woodland for 30 swine render. The Mauditts held the manor for nearly 200 years, and it was during their tenure that a Norman church was built. Its simple interior still engenders a sense of calm.

After the Mauditts, the manor passed to the Beauchamps, later to the de Chaworths (ancestors of none other than King Henry IV), and then to the Stuart family. In 1660, Nicholas Stuart became the first Baronet of Hartley Mauditt, possibly because he defended the manor against invading Roundheads during the English Civil War. Finally, the estate was acquired by the Stowell family, whose master preferred bustling town life to the quiet of Hartley Mauditt. The house was demolished and parts such as the staircase were repurposed at other estates.

However, the church may not be entirely deserted. Visitors have spoken of enchanting music drifting from it and of an eerie apparition – a phantom horse carriage racing the drive.

Address St Leonard's Church, Hartley Mauditt, GU34 3BP | Getting there Take bus 64 to Chawton, then bus 13 to Three Horseshoes, then a 30-minute walk | Hours Accessible 24 hours | Tip After your walk, have a refreshing drink at the bar of The Three Horseshoes hotel.

38 Hat Fair

The UK's longest-running Festival of Outdoor Arts

David Bowie's melancholic 'Starman' blasts from the loudspeaker onto the High Street as George Orange lifts his right foot off the metallic half-moon construction. Shifting his weight on his other leg, his entire balance now rests on a thin black rope that spans from one side of the rocking half-moon to the other. The audience gasps as the performer makes his way at lofty height across the rope, clapping frenetically as he reaches the other side. Yet, George Orange is not quite done. Still standing on the thin rope, he positions a large clown shoe on a wooden, L-shaped stick, lifts it up, takes the short end of the stick between his teeth and now balances not only himself but the shoe as well. The audience erupts with excitement – and not for the last time today.

For one day (sometimes three) in July, the historic streets and relaxing green spaces of Winchester turn raucous and rich in colour when thousands of people flock to the city centre to attend the UK's longest-running Festival of Outdoor Arts, the Winchester Hat Fair.

In 1974, only a year after Jonathan Kay launched the first ever Hat Fair in Covent Garden, the founder took the festival to Winchester. While the event in London had to stop due to scheduling reasons, it has continued in the Hampshire city ever since. The name derives from the custom of buskers passing around hats for the audience to leave a token of their appreciation after the performance.

Harvey Juggling, the artist who captivated his audience with knife juggling a few hundred metres away from George Orange, and who has performed not only at Covent Garden but at festivals like the Edinburgh Fringe and Glastonbury, recognises a unique atmosphere in Winchester. 'For once, we are the main attraction. The audience listens to everything you say and that is just beautiful.'

Address Hat Fair, Winchester City Centre, The Broadway, SO23 9GH, www.hatfair.co.uk | Getting there Various locations in the city centre | Hours Takes place early in July (with a break in 2026) – see the website for details | Tip Abbey Gardens, where a lot of the acts perform, is a beautifully serene place to visit throughout the year.

39 Hattingley Valley

Adding the sparkle to English wine

When Simon Robinson planted his first vine in 2008, he never imagined that less than two decades later, Hattingley Valley would be considered one of the most renowned English sparkling wines in the country, or that visitors would flock in groups to experience the winery firsthand through tours and tastings. But then again, he didn't yet know how grapes love to surprise.

In the early 2000s, as Simon looked to diversify his farm, he became intrigued by winemakers who had started producing sparkling wine using the traditional method. Could his land, Simon mused, do the same? After countless conversations and surveys, the first grapes – Chardonnay, Pinot Noir and Pinot Meunier, of course – were introduced, and nerve-wracking years followed.

'I kept looking at the vineyard,' Simon remembers. 'I wondered if there would be any grapes.' That was worry number one. In the end, the first harvest turned out to be rich and bountiful. But when it was time to try his first wine, Simon worried once more: 'Will this be drinkable?' Once again, he found himself pleasantly surprised: oh, it was fine indeed!

Finally... but a little sidenote first. In their first year of harvesting, Simon and his team collected about 400 or 500 kilograms of grapes – not enough in volume for the wine to be stored in a tank. Instead, they used an oak barrel. It was an emotional batch, of which he gifted some bottles to his goddaughter for her wedding.

During the wedding, he faced his third moment of worry. 'Will this variety taste alright?' It was flavoursome, he thought, but not spectacular. But then, 18 months later, Simon was invited to dinner at his goddaughter's and as she opened one of the leftover bottles, the group witnessed a transformation: the wine was fruity, creamy, fizzy; it was altogether perfect. This oak-fermented, well-rested sparkling wine is now Hattingley's premium product: the King's Cuvée.

Address Hattingley Valley Wine, Wield Road, Lower Wield, Alresford, SO24 9RX, www.hattingleyvalley.com | Getting there Take bus 64 to Alton, then bus 41 to Rushmore Lane, then a 10-minute walk | Hours Booking required for tours and tasting experiences (see website for details) | Tip After the tour, why not stop at the lovely pub The Yew Tree for refined English classics?

40 Hayward Guitars

Brian's string theory

Sometimes, Brian Hayward recognises the fault before the client has even stepped over the threshold. 'Buzzing at the 15th fret?' he asks, and the owner usually looks up in surprise. Brian then smiles. After nearly three decades of working as a luthier, he recognises the case immediately and knows this to be a common fault with this brand. In the sunlit workshop of his little garden studio, Brian Hayward gives broken string instruments new life. He sorts wiring problems, replaces damaged pieces, and mends guitars with broken necks and smashed bodies.

It started with his love for music – gentle blues, powerful rock, melancholy country music. 'When I was a kid, I used to play in lots of different bands,' he shares and his gaze wanders past the half a dozen guitars that are stored against the back of the workshop. 'I thought I would be a famous rock star.' He laughs. But then the pubs started closing, the work got harder, and Brian focused on his second passion. 'I love seeing when an instrument is no longer broken,' he says. 'When it can be enjoyed again. I like to think that maybe a next hit song is developed on it.' And just like that, his hobby became his full-time profession. These days, he repairs about 35 instruments a month.

But Brian Hayward doesn't just mend guitars, ukuleles, banjos and mandolins – he also builds them. Carefully, he takes a sleek electric guitar out of its casing. The red Padauk wood runs like silk beneath the fingers. After two years of dedicated work, he will soon be able to hand it over to its owner.

In 2025, his new album *Skeleton 52 (and Other Stories)* was released. It features 11 light yet emotional, punchy yet soft songs. They are written and composed by himself. For guitar luthier Brian Hayward hasn't given up his dream of becoming a rock star just yet.

Address Hayward Guitars, 5 West End Close, Winchester, SO22 5EW | Getting there A 13-minute walk from Winchester railway station | Hours By appointment only, Tue–Fri 10am–4pm, Sat 10am–1pm | Tip At the same premises, you can also view and purchase the wonderful landscape paintings of Clare Goodman.

41 High Street Clock

About time

Strolling through Winchester High Street, you will pass four public clocks within only four minutes. And while the clock on the New Guildhall is the tallest of these timepieces, the most iconic one sits further up the road. At number 49, an ornate wood-and-gold bracket projects over the street. The frame holds the High Street Clock – a timepiece whose origin lies in a small rivalry.

The story begins in 1712 when the original Guildhall was moved from its cramped chamber above the passageway next to the Buttercross – a route leading from the High Street to the cathedral – to the Old Market House up the road. That building was reconstructed with a modern ground floor to accommodate a covered market and an elegant façade featuring four flat arches and Doric stone columns. Following completion, Winchester MP George Rodney Brydges wanted to leave his mark – perhaps as a tribute to the city, possibly to help Winchester regain its former glory. He commissioned a statue of Queen Anne, which was placed in the central niche of the house. (If it was his goal to attract the attention of the monarchy, his efforts were in vain: after Queen Anne died in 1714, no other monarch showed any particular interest.) Brydges' act, however, drove fellow MP William Powlett to action. As Winchester's second representative, he potentially wanted to win back favour with the city's residents. He commissioned a public clock from the Huguenot clockmaker David Compigne. The intricate piece Compigne crafted, housed in its ornate wood-and-gold frame, was reportedly the first public clock in southern England to be illuminated by gas.

The people of Winchester seemed to appreciate Powlett's gesture: he was re-elected as MP in 1715. Brydges, on the other hand, did not live to see the success of his statue. He fell ill with gangrene after an ingrowing toenail only a year later.

Address High Street Clock, 49 High Street, Winchester, SO23 9BU | Getting there A 10-minute walk from Winchester railway station | Hours Accessible 24 hours | Tip You can find the world's oldest clock in the north nave of Salisbury Cathedral, 40 minutes from Winchester.

42 Highclere Castle

The real Earl and Countess of Downton Abbey

As you approach this imposing castle with its crowning towers and turrets, you might expect a familiar theme tune to start playing and for the Earl of Grantham (Hugh Bonneville) to appear. Ever since the British historical drama aired in 2010, the world has come to know the honey-hued manor as Downton Abbey. In reality, it is, of course, Highclere Castle, a beautiful Victorian stately home in north-western Hampshire.

Initially acquired by the Bishops of Winchester and rebuilt into a much grander home for the first time under Winchester College founder William of Wykeham in 1368, the impressive manor is home to the 8th Earl and Countess of Carnarvon. And they welcome not only film crews and wedding guests but also day visitors.

During guided tours, you can explore the opulent Double Library, which was even visited by Queen Elizabeth II, the Music Room (accessible through a hidden door from the library), and the ornate Drawing Room, a testament to Almina, the 5th Countess of Carnarvon, who transformed Highclere Castle into a hospital during World War I. You can marvel at the Saloon, which houses the huge Christmas tree in December, at the elegant Red Staircase – familiar to viewers as the route the Granthams rush down to attend a party – and get a glimpse into some of the 50 to 80 bedrooms. Then, just when you think there is nothing left to discover, you enter a whole new world in the basement: a vast Egyptian exhibition in honour of the 5th Earl of Carnarvon, who famously travelled with Howard Carter in the 1920s and helped discover the tomb of Tutankhamun.

Only beware. As you wander through the castle and its vast grounds (do not miss Jackdaw's Castle, the Etruscan Temple or the Temple of Diana), you might fall so in love with this England of décor and drama, of lavish balls and witty banter, that it will be hard to leave.

Address Highclere Castle, Highclere Park, Highclere, Newbury, RG20 9RN, www.highclerecastle.co.uk | **Getting there** A 26-minute car ride from Winchester city centre | **Hours** Advance booking required (see website for opening times) | **Tip** After visiting the castle, take your time to explore the gorgeous grounds of the estate. Rest under the enormous oak trees and soak in the abundance of nature.

43 Hockley Viaduct

Train to remain

When the military suggested blowing up Hockley Viaduct as part of their training in the 1980s, the idea did not go down well. The proposal sparked such controversy that the army ultimately had to back down. And indeed, it would have been a tragedy if these 33 elegant arches had fallen victim to a mere practice exercise.

Originally known as Shawford Viaduct, this structure was completed in the 1880s to bridge the River Itchen and its adjacent water meadows. It was designed to improve railway access from the Midlands via Didcot and Newbury to the Southampton Docks. This line then proved vital during both World Wars. Thousands of troops – including British, American and Canadian, Australian, Indian and Bermudian, Newfoundlander, Nova Scotian, Russian and Serbian – crossed the viaduct en route to and from military camps in Avington during World War I. During World War II, up to 16,000 trains crossed the railway bridge carrying military equipment towards the coast in the 12 months leading up to D-Day. But despite its wartime significance, the Didcot, Newbury and Southampton line did not become a commercial success. Passenger services had already ceased by the spring of 1960, and the line closed completely for goods four years later.

Today, you can catch a glimpse of the viaduct when you whizz (or more often creep) past on the M3 motorway. However, it's far more enjoyable to cross it on foot – it is very popular with runners – or on a bike, as it forms part of the National Cycle Route 23, which leads from Reading to Sandown on the Isle of Wight. And although you may think you are marvelling at a brick structure, do not be fooled: the viaduct conceals a concrete heart. That makes it not only one of the largest brick-built structures in Britain but also the oldest known viaduct in the country with a reinforced concrete core.

Address Hockley Railway Viaduct, Hockley Link, Compton, Winchester, SO21 2BD | Getting there A 13-minute walk from South Winchester Park & Ride | Hours Accessible 24 hours | Tip You can see traces of this railway heritage at the Chesil car park: the half-moon-shaped door on the left leads into the old railway tunnel, which once connected to the viaduct.

44 Horse and Rider

On the horseness of horses

If reproductions of art pieces served as portals, the High Street of Winchester would provide a swift passage to London's Bond Street. For the tactile bronze statue depicting a naked man sitting bareback on a bridle-less horse, located where the High Street meets Trafalgar Street since 1983, was not cast as one of its kind. The first statue was created in 1974 and is visible just opposite 180 Bond Street in the capital. The statues called *Horse and Rider* were created by the British artist Dame Elisabeth Frink.

Dame Elisabeth, who grew up in Suffolk and later lived in London, France and Dorset, was one of the most important sculptors of the 20th century. In her obituary, *The Times* stated that she had concentrated her work to capture 'the nature of Man', 'the "horseness" of horses', and 'the divine in human form'. Indeed, her large bronze statues are easily recognisable for their emotional details and their silent yet vibrant expressions.

Frink was born in November 1930, and her childhood was consumed by the terrors of World War II. As she grew up near an airbase, she would frequently hear the sounds of air raids and planes. It is the courage and simultaneous vulnerability of humans she must have felt only too strongly as a teenager, to which she dedicated herself to in her later work.

Although Dame Elisabeth cast many statues of humans and different animals, it is horses that stand out. Even in her childhood drawings, she focused on capturing the elegance of these animals. In the 1960s, when she moved with her second husband and her son to the south of France, she would observe local cowboys with their horses. After she was diagnosed with cancer in 1991, the horse became a symbol of strength as she created the larger-than-life statue of *War Horse*. And it was the statue of *Standing Horse* she was able to finish just before her death.

Address Horse and Rider, High Street, Winchester, SO23 9DF | **Getting there** An 8-minute walk from Winchester railway station | **Hours** Accessible 24 hours | **Tip** You can find various examples of Elisabeth Frink's work in the Dorset Museum in Dorchester, a 75-minute car ride from Winchester.

45 Hotel du Vin

Luxury, but make it cosy

Surely, a hotel can have no stronger seal of approval than counting the royal family among its former patrons – albeit, admittedly, their film doubles. When Netflix came to Winchester to film scenes for its hit series *The Crown* (the cathedral stood in for St Paul's Cathedral as well as Westminster Abbey), many cast members, General Manager Maria Forsberg recalls, stayed at Winchester's Hotel du Vin.

After all, this is a special branch of Britain's beloved boutique hotel chain. It was this elegant Georgian townhouse in the heart of Winchester that sommelier Gerard Bassett and hotelier Robin Hutson chose as their first ever Hotel du Vin in 1994. At a time when highbrow venues required a dress code and excluded children, Bassett and Hutson offered luxury as well as comfort – without the uncomfortably high price tag. Knowing that the details make the difference, they provided fresh milk in the minibar, swapped sheets and blankets for Egyptian cotton and made sure the showerheads were powerful. That same year, they opened a second venue in Birmingham's Jewellery Quarter.

While Winchester's popularity found an unconventional push in 1995 during the trial of serial killer Rosemary West (held in the adjacent Crown Court), more hotels soon followed: Bristol in 1999, and Tunbridge Wells in 2001. Two decades later, the chain boasts no fewer than 19 venues across the country.

As the name suggests, Hotel du Vin has never been just about a restful night's sleep – it's also about nourishing offerings. In the calm surroundings of soft lighting, elegantly framed portraits and restored fireplaces, you can enjoy buttery baked hake paired (as suggested) with a Sicilian Nero d'Avola, a classic afternoon tea and – the crown jewels that will never disappear from the menu – their crème brûlée.

Address Hotel du Vin & Bistro, 14 Southgate Street, Winchester, SO23 9EF | Getting there A 10-minute walk from Winchester railway station | Hours Hotel open daily, 24 hours; booking recommended for bistro | Tip During your stay, you might want to pop into the Everyman Cinema down the road for a cosy cinematic experience.

46 Hyde Abbey

The restless case of Alfred's last rest

Alfred the Great was not only the very first king with this epithet but also the monarch widely regarded as the first king of England (although, strictly speaking, such a title did not yet exist in the 9th century). Thus, you might expect his remains to be well preserved. Quite the opposite is true: we don't really know where they are.

Initially, Alfred was buried in Old Minster, the imposing church at the site of today's cathedral. However, before his death, he had ordered a new church to be built – a final resting place for the royal family. Once his son had fulfilled this wish, Alfred's remains were exhumed and re-interred at the new monastery. Alas, the peace was not to last: Old and New Minster were so close to one another that the voices of their choirs merged into inharmonious cacophony. New Minster needed a new home. A place just north of the city was found, and in 1110 the remains of King Alfred, his wife Ealhswith and his son Edward were dug up and re-buried at Hyde Abbey.

Today, only a stone gatehouse remains of the monastery that once encompassed several acres. The abbey suffered damage in 1141 when Winchester was burned during the civil war known as The Anarchy. But its final opponent was Henry VIII. In 1538, the abbey was dissolved, the building disassembled and the monastery soon forgotten.

Since then, the mystery of Alfred's remains has intrigued historians. In 1866, antiquarian John Mellor claimed to have found bones of the royal family. He sold them for 10 shillings, and they were re-interred at nearby St Bartholomew's Church. In 1999, the fragment of a pelvic bone was found, and after complex analysis it was concluded that it belonged to King Edward, his brother Æthelweard or King Alfred. Not wholly satisfying, you might say. But perhaps it's pleasing to imagine that the founder of Winchester was laid to rest in not just one place, but several places across this city.

Address Hyde Abbey, King Alfred Place, Winchester, SO23 7DF | **Getting there** A 10-minute walk from Winchester railway station | **Hours** Accessible 24 hours | **Tip** Curious about Alfred's final journey? Visit Winchester offers a free walking tour tracing his footsteps from the Broadway to the Abbey (www.visitwinchester.co.uk/business-directory/city-walk).

47_The Hyde Tavern

Where time just slips away

Some thresholds carry a distinct promise. As the strumming of a guitar softly echoes through the quiet street and the warm light spills from the two square windows, you sense it even before you open the heavy wooden door: this is a good place!

It wasn't always like that. In 2007, Janet Theodore arrived to help out at her daughter Ruth's request. The rustic pub with its low ceiling, wood panelling and large fireplace, though cosy, was run down, littered with cigarette stains and frequented by a group of men who had frightened the other regulars away. But in spite of, or maybe because of, the neglect, Janet was hooked. After teaching at Winchester Prison for the previous 20 years, she was looking for a change, and maybe also a challenge; she wanted to create a pub that was more like a community centre, where everyone felt comfortable – no trouble, no swearing and no drunken behaviour. Coincidentally, the former tenants were ready to step back and, only a year later, Janet Theodore was the landlady of The Hyde Tavern.

Within months, she turned the venue around: she redecorated, invited live musicians, and allowed people to bring in takeaway food (for a £1 charge) to accompany their drinks. She established a yearly beer festival (usually on Father's Day weekend) as well as an annual pie competition, which grew from eight contestants in the first year to thirty at its third event, making as much as £1,000 in 2025, to be donated to charity. In the little back room, various community groups meet on different days of the week, and ticketed events are held in a small performance space in the basement. No matter what day of the week, as you step through the old wooden door, you will be enveloped in a warm welcome. Accepting a pint or glass of your choice from Janet, you might find a little corner seat. If it is a Saturday, Rick Tarrant's strumming will calmly filter through the soft buzz of chatter and as you take your first sip, you can let time slip away for a while.

Address The Hyde Tavern, 57 Hyde Street, Winchester, SO23 7DY | Getting there An 8-minute walk from Winchester railway station | Hours Mon–Thu 6–11pm, Fri 6pm–midnight, Sat 3–11pm, Sun 3–7pm | Tip Looking for a lovely nearby restaurant that offers takeaway? Try the delicious dishes on offer at Lebanese House, in City Road.

48 Incognito

Let's party at John's House

Chadwick Smithfield, in case you are not yet aware, is the kind of cat that enjoys the finer things in life: Champagne for breakfast, a marvellous bubble bath 'after a long week of ducking and diving' and Mr Chow's famous Dragon Elixir, which cures even the meanest of hangovers. Even more: this sophisticated cat, with its elegant top hat, is not only a collector of refinements, but he is also eager to share them with others of similarly exquisite taste. For this, however, it is essential you are acquainted. After all, Chadwick Smithfield does not permit just anybody into his chambers.

Indeed, only the smallest of logos indicates that you are on the right track, as you reach the inconspicuous-looking wooden door on the side of St John's House on Broadway. It is a fitting venue. Not just because the historic stone walls present the ideal backdrop for an extravagant bar but also because the former hospital of St John's House once hosted the city's Assembly Rooms. In 1751, a ballroom was added on the first floor above the hospital wards; a grand place, where great musicians like Niccolò Paganini and Franz Liszt performed and, rumour has it, Jane Austen even attended a dance.

Opening the wooden side door, you are led to the souterrain below the ballroom, into a truly magical world of Incognito's very first speakeasy bar. (Later, venues in Kingston and Windsor followed.) Flickering candles and the subdued light of colourful lampshades illuminate opulent gilded frames depicting Chadwick and his friends. An exclusive bar that serves drinks so surreal you could never even have imagined them: Breakfast at Chadwick comes in a silver teapot, Along For The Ride is accompanied by a turning and blinking Ferris wheel, The Holy Grail is set on fire, and Mr Chow's Dragon doesn't just breathe smoke – its sharp, bitter flavours leave you breathless.

Address St John's House, The Broadway, Winchester, SO23 9BE | **Getting there** A short walk from Winchester bus station | **Hours** Wed & Thu 4pm–1am, Fri 3pm–2am, Sat noon–2am, Sun 2pm–midnight | **Tip** If you enjoy fine cocktails in an exquisite atmosphere, do visit the superb Greens Bar and Kitchen on Jewry Street.

49__The Ivy Winchester

Dining like it's 1917

Dark green may be a colour of camouflage, but chances are you know the façade of Winchester's Ivy restaurant opposite the Buttercross on the High Street even if you have never set foot inside. The square tables outside always neatly set; the iconic golden letters catch your eye, invite you in. And stepping in you should: let the bright colours and decor dazzle, the rich leather seating soothe, and the famous stained glass windows excite you – just like in the West End original.

In 1917, the young Italian Abel Giandolini opened a little café in London's West Street and was soon joined by Mario Gallati as maître d'. With their charm and culinary flair, they established the original Ivy, London's first theatreland restaurant. In its iconic triangular-shaped premises, it became famous for its Shepherd's Pie, the Traditional Fish and Chips and radiant atmosphere, frequented by none other than Elizabeth II and Winston Churchill.

More than a century later, the Ivy still knows how to charm – and no longer only in London. Since entrepreneur Richard Caring took over in the mid 2000s, the company has opened 46 spin-offs. In 2018, a central venue on Winchester's High Street, formerly housing an LK Bennett store, became one of them. While you will find all the classics – the Crispy Duck Salad, the Cured Salmon – there are local treasures, too: the King Alfred's Words cocktail turns heads with its thin layer of scarlet – the colour of blood, of power, of royalty – floating on top. As you take the first bite of your tender cod, only one question remains: how did the restaurant get its name? As with all good places, it comes with a dash of folklore.

'Don't worry,' actress Alice Delysia is said to have declared to a young Abel Giandolini as the restaurant owner apologised for inconvenience caused by building work in the house: 'We will always come and see you. We cling together like Ivy.'

Address The Ivy Winchester, 103–104 High Street, Winchester, SO23 9AH | **Getting there** A 9-minute walk from Winchester railway station | **Hours** Mon–Wed 8.30am–11pm, Thu & Fr 8.30am–noon, Sat 9am–midnight, Sun 9am–10.30pm | **Tip** If you enjoy the décor and style of The Ivy, pop into The Hambledon, a few metres away in The Square, for a lovely selection of floral interiors.

50 Jane Austen Statue

A depiction of strength and moral vision

On the count of three, actor Adrian Lukis (famous for his role as Mr Wickham in the BBC adaptation of *Pride and Prejudice*) and Winchester Cathedral's interim dean Reverend Canon Dr Roland Riem, pulled the white cord. The red cloth fell away and to the delighted gasps and excited applause of the surrounding audience, the sculpture was unveiled on a cloudy October day in 2025.

In the celebratory year of Jane Austen's 250th anniversary, Winchester wanted to pay fitting tribute to the great author. For such an endeavour only the most skilful artist would do. Thus, Winchester commissioned sculptor Martin Jennings, the acclaimed British artist who had also had the honour of designing and modelling the King Charles III head in profile for the Royal Mint in 2022, and had also been chosen to create a statue for Queen Elizabeth II.

While sculpting likenesses of monarchs demands exceptional technical ability, creating a sculpture of Jane Austen posed a different challenge as there are no uncontested portraits of the literary heroine. 'It was really baffling how to do this,' the artist told the *Hampshire Chronicle* on the day of the unveiling, 'because we base what little we know of what she looked like on a very brief sketch by her sister Cassandra – all other portraits are contested.' Working with this limited evidence, Jennings designed a sculpture highlighting the strength and moral vision of an author not only ahead of her time but whose appeal endures across centuries.

The statue, standing in the Inner Cloister of the Cathedral, depicts an elegant figure of five feet six inches (which was her approximate height). Jane wears typical Regency attire and a cap, under which a couple of ringlets have escaped. With her head held high, as she leans against her small writing table, there is an authoritative expression in her gaze that we should, perhaps, see far more often in female statues.

Address Jane Austen Statue, 9, Cathedral Close, The Close, SO23 9LS | Getting there A 7-minute walk from Winchester bus station | Hours Accessible 24 hours | Tip You might find a second-hand copy of an Austen novel at the nearby Deanery Bookstall.

51 Jane Austen's House

Scratching with secret pens in hidden corners

It is a truth universally acknowledged that an author of great importance would be in possession of a grand desk. Especially if this author pioneered a brand-new genre of writing. Yet, when you enter the dining room of the cottage in Chawton – where Jane Austen lived with her mother and her sister Cassandra from 1809 to 1817 and wrote, edited and published all six of her novels – you find a summer-hat-sized, 12-sized walnut tripod table tucked back next to the fireplace. It is on this fragile table, family tradition says, that Jane Austen would work quietly and discreetly, in a neat, tidy manner.

'She was careful,' her nephew James Edward Austen-Leigh observes in his *Memoir of Jane Austen*, 'that her occupation should not be suspected by servants, or visitors, or any persons beyond her own family party.' Indeed, James continues, '[she] wrote upon small sheets of paper which could easily be put away or covered with a piece of blotting paper.' After all, being an author wasn't a desirable profession for a woman at that time. Her manuscripts were submitted with secrecy, delivered by male relatives, printed without her name. Did she ever imagine that 50,000 visitors a year would flock to her former home?

On 23 July 1949, the cottage opened as a museum. After reading an advertisement by Chawton resident Dorothy Darnell in *The Times*, Mr Carpenter, a London solicitor whose son had died in the war, was moved to support the idea of honouring the great author. Jane Austen's novels had brought comfort to his son, as to many British soldiers: *Pride and Prejudice* was the most widely read book in the trenches during World War I and special editions of *Persuasion* and *Northanger Abbey* were distributed during World War II.

Eight years after the museum opened, Jane's writing table was moved into the house once more. It is now the object that visitors are most eager to see.

Address Jane Austen's House, Winchester Road, Chawton, GU34 1SD, www.janeaustens.house/visit/visitor-info | Getting there Take bus 64 from Winchester to Chawton Roundabout | Hours See website for seasonal openings | Tip Finish your visit with a refreshing cream tea from Cassandra's Cup just across the road from the museum.

52 Jane Austen's Last Home

Where humour and her sister's love never left her

Few sibling bonds are as close as that between Jane and Cassandra Austen. The sisters spent most of their days together and, when apart, corresponded frequently. Thus, when Jane's health began to decline and it was decided she should move from Chawton to Winchester to be closer to doctor Dr Giles Lyford, Cassandra accompanied her eagerly. In May 1817, they arrived to take lodgings at 8 College Street. 'We have,' Jane wrote in a letter to her nephew James Edward Austen-Leigh, 'a neat little drawing-room with a bow window overlooking Dr. Gabell's garden.'

Even in waning health, Jane's passion for writing remained undiminished. On 15 July (St Swithun's Day, which coincided with the fashionable Winchester Races), she began drafting a witty poem. Perhaps it was a nod to lighter days; the Austen family often wrote playful verses as part of parlour games or to commemorate family events. In the poem, Jane imagined that the 'good people' of Winchester had forgotten to seek 'the leave of St Swithin' before holding the races. Offended, St Swithun vowed to 'triumph in shewing my powers', declaring if the races were not shifted, 'The curse upon Venta is July in showers'. ('Venta Belgarum' was the old Roman name for Winchester). This poem was the last work Jane Austen composed. She died three days later, on 18 July 1817, her head resting in Cassandra's lap.

It was also at 8 College Street that the sisters were finally parted. Women rarely attended funerals in that era, so Cassandra followed Jane's funeral procession to Winchester Cathedral from the window of their lodging. 'I watched,' Cassandra wrote in a letter to her niece Fanny, 'the little procession the length of the street & when it turned from my sight… I had lost her for ever.'

Today, the house is owned by Winchester College. In 2025, it was opened to the public for the first time.

Address Jane Austen's Last Home, 8 College Street, Winchester, SO23 9LX | **Getting there** A 10-minute walk from Winchester bus station | **Hours** Viewable from the outside only | **Tip** If you want to trace Jane Austen's steps in Winchester, in 2025 the visitor information centre created a Jane Austen Trail through the city.

53 Keats' Walk

Find inspiration for your ode

'This Winchester,' John Keats told his girlfriend Fanny Brawne in a letter on 16 August 1819, 'is a fine place.' Excitedly he wrote that he had been able to change his 'little coffin of a room' at Shanklin for a larger chamber that 'looks out onto a beautiful – blank side of a house. It is strange,' he continued, 'I should like it better than the view of the sea from our window at Shanklin.'

Keats had arrived with his friend Charles Brown from the Isle of Wight in search of libraries. But while Winchester back then offered the Morley Library as well as the Fellows' Library at Winchester College, it is unlikely these were within the means of the young poets. This fact did not keep Keats from falling in love with the town, the soft hills and the gently flowing streams surrounding it. So, it was in Winchester while experiencing the 'season of mists and mellow fruitfulness' that he crafted the now most anthologised poem in the world: *To Autumn*.

To follow in the footsteps of the great poet, make your way to the Guildhall. Either obtain a Keats' Walk leaflet from the Visitor Information Centre or download it from www.visitwinchester.co.uk. Start your walk by turning left onto the High Street and take the second left into Market Street towards the cathedral. Jane Austen had been buried there two years prior to Keats' visit, and the poet would stroll through the nave perusing the letters of his girlfriend, Fanny. The walk continues through Cathedral Close into College Street and past Winchester College (with the unattainable library). Tracing the stone wall of the college, you will reach the path through the water meadows. Saunter past the clear chalk stream with its vibrant crowfoot and dancing starworts until you reach the Gothic towers of Hospital St Cross. Follow Keats' last instruction of passing 'across St Cross meadows till you come to the most beautifully clear river'.

Address Keats' Walk spans approximately two miles. Start at Winchester Guildhall, The Broadway, Winchester, SO23 9GH | Getting there The Guildhall is a 15-minute walk from Winchester railway station | Hours Accessible 24 hours | Tip Why not stop for refreshment at The Bell Inn near Hospital St Cross on the way home?

54 Kingsgate Books & Prints

Mapping out the ancient city walls

A little shop, hidden inside thick city walls? Tucked away in a (then) calm side street at the back of the cathedral? 'What are you thinking?' people asked when Mike Fowkes shared his idea in 1991. 'This is never going to last.' More than three decades later, he has proved you must not listen to the doubters when you have a vision.

These days, as a steady stream of visitors wanders along Dome Alley through Prior's Gate, many pause in charmed reverence at the sight of the elegantly arched bay window, the white-washed window frame set against scarlet red walls and – behind the glass – beautifully crafted maps of Winchester, Hampshire and other parts of the world. Tucked into the left corner of one of Winchester's two surviving medieval city gates (the other being Westgate), Mike Fowkes runs one of the city's most distinctive shops: Kingsgate Books & Prints.

Thousands of cartographic works from various centuries, in different sizes and created with various means, are stacked, lined up or hung in the densely packed little room. 'You would not guess that I am actually a minimalist,' he says, grinning. Having specialised in rare prints – like the 224-year-old copper-engraved radius map that sits prominently in the window on the day of the visit – he has attracted the interest of former Prime Ministers (not just the one who went to school in nearby Winchester College), of Hollywood stars and even of the royal family. 'I always had a passion for maps,' Mike Fowkes says. 'They teach us so much more than just geography. They tell us about history, about world views, about beliefs.'

There is only one potential downside to a shop inside a medieval gate: there is no possibility of central heating. Yet, even on winter days you will find the shop's door wide open. Mike Fowkes explains: 'I am rather cold and welcoming than comfortable but detached.'

Address Kingsgate Books & Prints, Kingsgate Street, Winchester, SO23 9PD, www.kingsgatebooksandprints.co.uk | Getting there A 9-minute walk from Winchester bus station | Hours See website for opening hours, which vary | Tip The books and prints shop is not the only inviting entity within Kingsgate. On the other side, you find the steps leading up to St Swithun-upon-Kingsgate.

55 The Kite Flyer

Bringing paper to Parchment Street

Having yearly exhibitions to prepare, the British artist Marzia Colonna doesn't usually have the capacity to undertake commissions. However, when Winchester City Council was looking for a public artwork in Winchester's Parchment Street to attract more trade into this charming road, she could not miss this opportunity. After all, one of her sons lived at this very address. But what sculpture could elevate the street the best, she wondered. Marzia decided she wanted to honour the name, parchment. A memory of her childhood returned: her father crafting delicate kites out of paper and bamboo, the kites dancing in the wind; light, gentle, joyful. 'In a world full of plastic toys and expensive things,' Marzia explains, 'kites are a symbol of carefree happiness.' But where to position it? Well, there was only one spot that would not only be right for a kite flier but also ideal in this narrow inner-city street: high up.

The idea convinced the city council as well as the residents. With the assistance of a structural engineer, who ensured the safety of the artwork, Marzia crafted a statue in wax before sending it to be cast in bronze, while the bridge and the kites were being manufactured by Denmead's Metal Art Design. On Sunday 5 April 2009, it was time. With the help of a crane, the kite flier on its bridge was to be positioned, six metres above the ground. 'I had nightmares,' Marzia admits. 'There was this enormous crane dangling over the bridge. It was like when you take a shelf out of a fridge, and you are worried whether you will get it in again.' But everything fitted perfectly.

This kite flier – playful, iconic, yet light – turned out to be particularly poignant for some: 'A lady who lives in Parchment Street got in touch,' Marzia recounts. 'Her husband was terminally ill and flying a kite was one of the items on his bucket list.' As they returned from a weekend away, the new statue felt like a mini miracle. 'This kite flier,' the lady wrote, 'will forever hold a special place in my heart.'

Address The Kite Flier, Parchment Street, Winchester, SO23 8AT | Getting there A 7-minute walk from Winchester bus station | Hours Accessible 24 hours | Tip Just next to the sculpture (on the ground level) there is the super cute Audrey's Tearoom.

56 Lainston's Lime Trees

The avenue that charms world leaders

The Delft Suite offers one of the most stunning hotel room views in Hampshire. Upon entering the bedroom, the gaze travels to the tall middle window. There, in a perfectly straight line, a sweeping avenue runs three-quarters of a mile down the hill. Flanked by the bulbous crowns of lime trees, this so-called *gentleman's vista* is the longest avenue of linden trees to be found in England. It's no surprise that former Prime Minister Margaret Thatcher chose this very room to stay in while working on her memoirs.

Nestled into greenery, Lainston House is a grand 17th-century manor turned luxury hotel. Rumour has it that even King Charles II stayed here with his mistress Louise de Kérouaille. In the back garden, you can see the remains of a 12th-century chapel. It was here that Elizabeth Chudleigh is said to have secretly married naval officer Augustus Hervey in 1744 (as Maid of Honour to the Prince of Wales this would have been forbidden). With Augustus at sea, their bond quickly broke and 25 years later, Elizabeth remarried – this time to Sir Evelyn Pierrepont, 2nd Duke of Kingston-upon-Hull – in a pompous ceremony. But her past caught up with her: when the duke died, leaving her his fortune, his nephew contested the will and accused Elizabeth of bigamy. When she was found guilty by the House of Lords, she fled England to the Continent – taking her fortune with her.

A portrait of Elizabeth Chudleigh can today be found in the first-floor hallway of Lainston House. The staff treat it with caution. Years ago, when the portrait (then displayed in the restaurant downstairs) was taken off for cleaning, a large mirror, fixed tightly to the wall, suddenly crashed to the floor. It was promptly rehung. Later, when the restaurant was renovated, the painting was – carefully! – relocated to a wall overlooking the oval green. This time, no mirrors moved. Elizabeth, the staff concluded, approved of her new placement.

Address Lainston House, Woodman Lane, Sparsholt, Winchester, SO21 2LT | **Getting there** Take bus 7 from City Road Stop to Sparsholt Turning, then an 18-minute walk | **Hours** The hotel area is open to residents only, but the restaurants are open to non-patrons (booking recommended) | **Tip** If you want to stretch your legs, there are lovely walks from Lainston House to the nearby village of Sparsholt.

57 The Lavender Fields

Violet dreams at Hartley Park Farm

On a sunny summer's day, Provence can be found at the back of Hartley Park Farm, nestled between Alton and Selborne. Stepping into the sunlit barn, a wonderfully sweet, slightly woody and deeply herbaceous scent wraps itself around you. And while lavender oils as well as lavender creams, and lavender latte as well as lavender Earl Grey teas, tempt you from the left and right corners of the shop, your eyes are probably drawn straight ahead. Through the back door and the large windows, you can already glimpse the indulgent bushes of dusty violet blossoms on sage-green stems that spill in neat rows down the field. You have reached the Lavender Barn.

In 1999, the Butler family put their metaphorical eggs into a completely new, violet-coloured basket. Originally, like many farmers in Hampshire, they had been growing hops. But changes in drinking habits and import competition had caused a sharp decline in the hop industry since the 1980s. Following the advice of the British Hop Association – which encouraged farmers to focus on crops useful for essential oils like mint or coriander – the Butlers focused on lavender.

A quarter of a century later, their decision has been pioneering. Today, people don't just frequent the farm shop for lavender products, the fields themselves have turned into a tourist attraction. Up to 15,000 visitors rush to the farm during the eight weeks between mid June and mid August, ambling between the neat rows, taking one (or a couple of dozen) pictures. Welcoming thousands of visitors brings its quirks. Over the years, Nick and Lyndsay Butler have also received unusual requests, from people asking to pose nude among the lavender to others who wondered whether they could park their car in the middle of the lavender field. They take it in good humour, viewing it as part of the charm of sharing their farm with the public.

Address The Lavender Barn, Hartley Park Farm Business Centre, Selborne Road, Alton, GU34 3HP | Getting there Take bus 64 to Chawton and then bus 38 to Hartley Park Farm, then a 5-minute walk | Hours Mid Jun–mid Aug (lavender season): Mon–Sat 10am–5pm, Sun 10am–4pm; outside lavender season: farm shop and café Tue–Sat 10am–5pm; closed Jan | Tip Before you head back, stop at The Rose & Crown pub in the utterly charming nearby village of Upper Farringdon.

58 Licoricia Statue

A woman worth remembering

In the 1200s, when women's economic stability relied heavily on the goodwill of their fathers, husbands or brothers, Licoricia of Winchester, a twice-widowed single mother of five children, was so successful, she mingled with the royal court. She was the most important Jewish woman in Winchester and maybe even the most influential British woman of her time. But although news of her death in 1277 travelled as far as Germany, the case of her murder was never solved.

By 1234, Licoricia lived with four children in Winchester. Her first husband Abraham had died, and she had become a moneylender in her own terms. Moneylending was one of the few professions open to Jews at that time (as it was considered sinful by Christians) and Licoricia was very successful at it – maybe so successful she attracted the attention of David of Oxford, one of the most prominent English Jews of the 13th century. So keen was he to marry Licoricia that he endured a complex legal battle to divorce his first wife Muriel. But David died only two years after their marriage (and the birth of their son Asher) – and Licoricia was imprisoned in the Tower of London. It was custom for the king to seize one third of a Jewish person's property after they had died and to imprison the heirs so they couldn't interfere in the process. Eventually, King Henry III took 5,000 marks (£3 million in today's money) and used it to help fund the rebuilding of Westminster Abbey.

Despite the lost money and the more challenging times for the Jewish community, Licoricia continued her thriving business – until 1277, when her daughter Belia discovered her and her maid brutally stabbed to death, possibly during a robbery. Although various men were accused of theft, the murderer was never found. Since 2022, a statue of Licoricia together with her son Asher, in front of The Arc, has commemorated the Jewish businesswoman.

Address In front of The Arc, Jewry Street, Winchester, SO22 6RX | Getting there A 5-minute walk from Winchester railway station | Hours Accessible 24 hours | Tip Follow the self-guided Jewish Medieval Trail through Winchester and learn more about Winchester's rich Jewish heritage (see www.visitwinchester.co.uk).

59 Linocuts with Depth

Crafting sessions that soothe the soul

You recognise the sights immediately: the grand West Window of the cathedral, the sharp spikes of the Buttercross, the proud statue of the city's founder holding his down-pointing sword up high. The designs on tea towels and cards neatly arranged on Kristina's kitchen countertop are so realistic they could be photographs. In reality, Kristina J Smith has designed them by carefully carving tiny lines with gouges into linoleum.

For a beginner who hasn't touched a paint brush since school (and remembers craft lessons with mixed feelings), these designs inspire a sense of unreachable awe. And yet, Kristina is confident that by the end of this workshop, one will leave with a similar design of one's own.

As an artist, Kristina had long focused on oil paintings and sketches. So, at first, she was sceptical when her husband brought home the lino printing kit. 'I thought it's a bit crafty, a bit processy,' she says as she lays out the pencils, pieces of soft lino and U-shaped carving tools. 'But the moment I pulled my first print, I was sold.'

At the beginning, the printing was something she did for herself – channelling her old creativity, finding stillness in the hectic pace of everyday life. But when she ran out of friends to gift her cards to, somebody asked why she wasn't selling them. In a natural transition, that question led to the intimate workshops she has been offering for the last couple of years. In an age when teenagers and adults spend more and more time scrolling on their phone, Kristina invites them to create rather than look at creators. 'Take your time,' she suggests. 'If you guide the Pfeil carving tool more slowly, you can work more accurately.' The card, carefully wrapped and slipped into the bag at the end, indeed looks surprisingly professional. But more than that: in between the slower movements, the cups of tea and the soft questions, a calmness has set in, which hasn't been felt for some time.

Address Kristina J Smith Prints, Tees Farm Road, Colden Common, SO21 1UQ, kristinajsmithprints.setmore.com | Getting there Bus 69 to Primary School, Colden Common, then a 5-minute walk | Hours Booking essential (see website for details) | Tip If you would like to purchase rather than create prints, you can find Kristina's tea towels and cards in the Winchester Tourist Information Centre and Hampshire Pantry.

60 Lower Norton Flower Farm

A garden of dazzling friends

Here are the roses, fabulous ones. Over there, the dahlias, the big show-offs. And along the border at the far end, the romantics: cosmos, honeysuckle and hollyhocks. Strolling with Alison Coleman through her flower field feels like being acquainted with a group of dazzling, if slightly quirky friends. Passing tall bushes with blossoms of blushing peach, deep raspberry and dramatic cerise, one cannot help but sigh with relief. Whatever stress waits outside, within these two acres of bloom, the world feels soothing.

In 2021, Alison gave herself the push to transform part of her arable farm into what she loved the most: flowers. She started slowly, planting the first bulbs in the former vegetable patch next to the barn; thinking she might be able to sell a few posies in jars to neighbours. But in the first year alone, demand was so high that the horses had to be moved to another field to make room for expanding flower borders.

Five years on, together with her small but mighty team, Alison grows perennials and annuals, roses and shrubs, for foliage. 'It was a steep learning curve,' the flower farmer admits. 'I have discovered a thousand ways to kill a plant.' She laughs, her gaze travelling across the field with admiration. 'I am very much a trial-and-error girl.'

In her fields, visitors can now either pick their own flowers or, if they want a little bit more guidance, join one of their garden tours. For those feeling creative, there are various workshops: dried flower frames, vase arrangements or wreath making (beware, the Christmas ones especially sell out fast).

Entering the spacious Flower Barn, a bouquet of floral sweetness fills your nose. At the back, bunches of strawflowers in every shade hang to dry and the large wooden table beckons you to take a seat and lose yourself in the sweetest pastime of all: crafting with nature.

Address Lower Norton Flower Farm, Sutton Scotney, SO21 3NE, www.lowernortonflowerfarm.com | Getting there Take bus 75 to Lower Bullington Turn, then a 17-minute walk | Hours Advance booking required (see website for workshop schedule) | Tip The nearby Norton Park Manor Hotel offers lovely spa breaks and great afternoon tea.

61 The Manor of God Begot

How Queen Emma ruled them all

With its dark timber framing against the whitewashed walls, its two sharp gables and the projecting bay windows, God Begot House is hard to miss as you stroll along Winchester's High Street. But did you know that this site once housed a royal residence?

In 1012, 12 years after the wedding of King Æthelred to Queen Emma, Æthelred II made his wife another gift: the Manor of God Begot (then known as Goudbeyete). Although located within the city walls, this residence was not subject to Winchester's civic regulations. Instead, the manor held its own legal privileges, exempt from the mayor of Winchester as well as, remarkably, the king himself. It was a fitting gift for a powerful woman: Queen Emma was not only married to two kings (making her the only English queen to be crowned twice) but also mother of two more sovereigns from rivalling dynasties, and became one of the most influential political figures of the 11th century.

Initially to secure an allegiance against invading Vikings, Emma was sent from Normandy to England to marry King Æthelred II. However, when her husband died in London 14 years later – while under threat from Danish King Cnut – newly widowed Emma allied herself with the victor. Far from being compelled, Emma was astute in navigating the powers of politics and on Cnut's side, she became the wealthiest woman in England. After the death of her second husband (and the brief reign of his son, Harold Harefoot), Emma's son Harthacnut took to the throne. He was succeeded only two years later by Emma's other son, Edward the Confessor.

When Emma died in 1052, she left the manor to the monks of St Swithun's Priory, who continued to enjoy its privileges – until the Dissolution of the Monasteries under Henry VIII. Today, as home to a branch of Ask Italian, the house serves pizza and pasta, but its stones still whisper of monks and queens.

Address God Begot House, 101 High Street, Winchester, SO23 9AH | **Getting there** A 10-minute walk from Winchester railway station | **Hours** Accessible 24 hours | **Tip** The Royal Blood Trail marks the connections between the places in the city that have featured in royal visits and events from the Saxon era to the present day (see www.visitwinchester.co.uk for details).

62 Market Lane Toilets

No need to (be) flush to visit this museum

For an educational hub such as Winchester – home to not only the oldest, continuously running school but also one of the grandest cathedrals in the country – it should come as no surprise that even a public toilet has its own little museum.

As you approach the red brick building in Market Lane just at the exit of a little passage connecting the High Street via St Maurice's Covert, you will not only spot the well-known male/female sign indicating a public convenience but also a two-storey display of curious sanitary artefacts behind a glass wall on the right-hand side of the toilet building. The little museum presents curious hygienic artefacts – from colourful Roman mosaics to medieval water aquamaniles (ceramic water jugs) found in latrine pits, an Edwardian flush system and a wooden sign that was once positioned to indicate the Gentlemen's room at the City Museum. For this innovative idea, Market Lane Toilets, when opened in 2006, won the Royal Institute of British Architects Award.

The artefacts stem from Winchester Museum's archive and are intended to encourage passersby to visit the nearby collection and explore Winchester's once complicated relationship with the Itchen River. While its chalk stream runs with pure, clear water today, without proper drainage, and with overflowing cesspits and soiled floors, the River Itchen had become so polluted by 1848 that there was an outbreak of cholera. As the wastewater ran downhill, the lowest areas like Parchment Street were worst affected. Yet the sensible arguments for a new, clean sewage system, and higher quality of life, made by those such as Dean Thomas Garnier, were drowned out by the cries of the so-called Muckabites, who prioritised the money in their pockets over public health. The issue was resolved via a national requirement for sanitation. In 1875, the main sewer was built. To this day, people know the lower part of Morestead Road – where the Pumping Station was erected – as Stink Pot Hill.

Address Market Lane, Winchester, SO23 | Getting there A 4-minute walk from Winchester bus station | Hours Daily 8.30am–6.30pm (1 May–30 Sep 8am–8pm) | Tip Visit the beautiful garden in the Cathedral Close, erected in honour of clean water proponent Dean Thomas Garnier.

63 Micheldever Wood

Fifty shades of blue (or violet, really)

Each year, at the beginning of April, a miracle occurs in the British countryside. Seemingly overnight, a misty carpet of vibrant violet, indigo, purple, iris, amethyst and mauve hues stretches over the forest floors. Indeed, around half of the world's bluebells grow in the United Kingdom.

One particularly lovely location where they bloom in the dappled shade of ancient woodland is located just seven miles northeast of Winchester: Micheldever Wood. To find the post, make your way to the car park on the country lane simply called *Main Road*. From there, turn right and follow a forest path for a few hundred metres before turning left and heading up the hill. Soon, the violet carpet that hovers in the distance becomes too intriguing to ignore.

No wonder bluebells are associated with fairy magic and enchantment. Does it not seem positively plausible that fairies used these spring flowers, with their delicate bell shapes, to summon their kin? And is it not fitting that, as a human, one should be cautious when hearing that sound? Would it not feel entirely likely that the sweet sight and scent of these blooms could bewitch adults and children alike? After all, even the novelist Emily Brontë called them 'sweetest flower / That waves in summer air'. And should you not take great care to avoid trampling one, lest you anger a fairy?

Incidentally, it would also be against the law. Under the Wildlife and Countryside Act 1981, it is prohibited to intentionally dig up, uproot or destroy wild bluebells or for landowners to remove and sell them. Bluebells are delicate creatures. Their soft, succulent leaves are particularly sensitive when crushed: if a leaf gets damaged, it can no longer absorb the sunlight or photosynthesise and thus dies, reducing the plants' ability to propagate.

But really, you would not want to incur the wrath of the fairies anyway.

Address Micheldever Wood car park, Main Road, Alresford, SO24 9TZ | Getting there A 19-minute drive from Winchester | Hours Accessible 24 hours | Tip You really should not leave before paying a visit to the nearby village Micheldever, strolling past the picture postcard cottages and having a snack at the Half Moon & Spread Eagle pub.

64 The Milbury at Beauworth

Listening in to Hampshire's deepest well

Clive Cummings bends his knees and tilts the little blue shovel in his right hand, and the chunky ice cubes tumble through the gaps in the cast-iron grate. They clatter against the walls on their way down, until – a full 10 seconds later – a deep, echoing *dong!* marks the impact on the water below. 'Three hundred feet,' Clive says as he straightens his legs, and as an onlooker you cannot help but nod admiringly.

Built in the early 12th century, this well – tucked away in a cosy *séparée* next to the bar in the historic pub The Milbury – is said to be the oldest in the country. To lower a bucket to the groundwater, a person must walk one mile on the 250-year-old human-powered turning wheel adjacent to the well and another mile to bring the bucket up again. 'We wanted to find a quintessentially English pub and when we saw this,' Clive says pointing at the well, 'we knew we had found our property. It is now our home, business, passion and... nightmare.' But he laughs as he says this, and it is clear he's enjoying the project.

On 11 April 2023, Clive and Tanith Cummings bought the 400-year-old pub on Salt Lane today known as The Milbury at Beauworth. After spending the previous 17 years in Burgundy, transforming the 13th-century Cistercian Abbaye de la Bussière into a luxury hotel complete with a Michelin star restaurant, they were ready to return home to England and nurture a new hospitality venture. At The Milbury, they offer refined English cuisine with a modern, Mediterranean twist. Food is served in tapas style, as soon as each dish is ready, which lends an unusually communal feeling to the dining experience.

The pub sits high on a hill to the east of Winchester. A small firepit helps guests linger through colder evenings in the charming garden and the stunning view north towards Beauworth and Hinton Ampner is admired almost as much as the spectacle of ice cubes tumbling down the well.

Address The Milbury, Beauworth, Alresford, SO24 0PB | **Getting there** 8 miles from Winchester railway station | **Hours** Wed–Sat noon–9pm, Sun noon–7pm | **Tip** Nearby Beacon Hill National Nature Reserve beckons to be explored either before or after the pub lunch.

65 Mint Tea Boutique

Where two friends help others succeed

The idea came, quite unexpectedly, during a girls' trip to Marrakech, celebrating a friend's birthday before she was to emigrate to Australia. Rebecca Hopkins and Louise Goodall, friends and work colleagues for decades, had both been made redundant and were tinkering with plans for the future. What if, the two young mothers thought, they didn't simply seek another job? What if, instead, they started their own business helping others shine?

Back in England, they went hunting for pockets of beauty: accessories, stationery, clothes, that could not be found in the high street chains, ideally from small businesses and sold at affordable prices. Their finds were shared at little parties in people's homes. 'Like,' Bex says, 'an old-fashioned Tupperware party.' The concept worked so well that they soon had to split up in order to meet demand. A shop in Westbourne followed, then one in Winchester's Southgate Street, before moving into their forever-shop-home: a two-storey corner shop in St Thomas Street.

Stepping inside, you find a fine collection from British creatives. There are the dainty necklaces handmade by Kerry, who was designing on the side when Bex and Lou met her and has since fully committed to her bohemian jewellery brand, Formation Co. Then, there are the soft cardigans and dresses from Sugarhill, designed by the siblings Pawel and Aleks in Brighton. And the charming cards by Frankie and Tom from 'You've Got Pen On Your Face', who, as they claim, spend 'an unhealthy amount of time' coming up with witty one-liners. Lou smiles as she puts the stack of cards back on the shelf.

It's been quite a journey for the two friends. Having moved from living room parties to several shop locations, the memory of the beginning always stays with them: those excited discussions on hot Marrakech nights, sipping mint tea and dreaming of what could be.

Address Mint Tea Boutique, 4 St Thomas Street, SO23 9HE | Getting there A 9-minute walk from Winchester bus station | Hours Mon–Sat 10am–5pm, Sun 11am–4pm | Tip If you're a fan of independent boutiques, you should also stop at Sass&Edge and H&B Style for clothes, and the Consortium for vintage furniture.

66 The Mizmaze

A soul's journey is never straight

Half an hour's stroll from the city centre, you will find a natural phenomenon that is the last of only two surviving examples in England. Follow the River Itchen, turn left after Garnier Road, and walk uphill until you meet the copse on the hilltop. Turn left again, trace the edges of the thicket and after a few moments you will spot a peculiar pattern in the grassy field ahead: the Winchester Mizmaze.

Mizmazes are turf labyrinths (of which eight still exist in England) but unlike conventional mazes they offer only a single path to the centre. The example on top of St Catherine's Hill, however, is even more unusual: it is not round but square in shape. The only other surviving mizmaze in England can be found 26 miles to the west, near Breamore House on the edge of the New Forest. While some believe Winchester's maze to be as much as 400 years old, local legend sets it in the 18th century and offers quite a dramatic backstory. According to the tale, a boy from Winchester College was sent to St Catherine's Hill as punishment for misbehaviour. Inspired by Greek mythology, he began to carve a winding path into the hilltop. But instead of finding calm, the twists and turns of the maze distressed him to such an extent that he hurled himself off the hill and drowned in the river.

Indeed, mazes have long appeared in myth and folklore; they may have been used for festivals, as Titania remembers in Shakespeare's *A Midsummer Night's Dream* 'the quaint mazes in the wanton green'. Yet, stepping into it and following the groove, another interpretation comes to mind. As the path winds and bends, leading to the outer corners of the labyrinth and then so close to the exit you think you have mastered it already only to be drawn away again, you cannot help but observe: 'This feels like the path of life.' And fittingly, in Christian symbolism, the labyrinth represents the soul's journey.

Address Winchester Mizmaze, St Catherine's Hill, Garnier Road, Winchester, SO23 9BN | Getting there Take the WPR bus to Winchester Park & Ride East, then a 10-minute walk | Hours Accessible 24 hours | Tip For a longer walk, follow the River Itchen southward until Shawford and treat yourself at the lovely Bridge Inn.

67_Nunnaminster

The mysterious miracles of St Edburga

During the Middle Ages, Winchester's three monasteries formed the largest concentration of religious houses north of the Alps. While the legacy of Old Minster lives on in the city's cathedral and the community of New Minster was relocated to Hyde Abbey, all that remains of Nunnaminster is a rectangular excavation site between the New Guildhall and Abbey Gardens. Yet, the story behind these ruins whispers of wonder and female worship.

Founded around 903 by Queen Ealswith, widow of Alfred the Great, Nunnaminster quickly became a prestigious centre of learning and the arts. The *Book of Nunnaminster* is not only one of the oldest surviving English prayer books but is also notable for using certain feminine grammatical forms, suggesting it may have been written by female scribes. Additionally, some of the earliest known examples of Anglo-Saxon embroidery were created here: a stole and a maniple given to the shrine of St Cuthbert in 934.

Arguably the most fascinating aspect of the monastery is the mystery around St Edburga, Ealswith's granddaughter. At the age of three, when presented with objects signifying worldly riches and religious practices, she chose a chalice. This her father interpreted as a divine sign: she must, he thought, be destined for life in a convent. Despite her royal lineage, she refused to be treated in a superior manner to her sisters. Instead, it is said she secretly cleaned their shoes and placed herself in the service of less experienced nuns. Edburga was also believed to have healing powers. In one account, a blind woman regained her sight after cleaning her eyes with water that Edburga had washed her hands in. After Edburga's death, the nuns reportedly found themselves unable to close the window beside her tomb. Interpreting this as a miracle, they began to believe in her sanctity. Twelve years later, Edburga was elevated to sainthood.

Address Nunnaminster, 2 Abbey Passage, Winchester, SO23 9LL | Getting there A short walk from Winchester bus station | Hours Accessible 24 hours | Tip If you are a freelancer and, like the nuns, crave a little community, the nearby Abbey Mill offers a lovely co-working space.

68_The Old Gaolhouse

Serving drinks, not time

JD Wetherspoon likes to settle in unusual places. On the Isle of Wight, in Leeds and Folkestone, the pub chain has opened branches in former churches; in Edinburgh, Glasgow and London, pubs have emerged in former banks; and in Tunbridge Wells, Llandudno and Edinburgh, Wetherspoon has converted cinemas and opera houses. But perhaps its darkest transformation is found in Winchester. On Jewry Street, Wetherspoon now serves customers where prisoners once served their time.

A prison existed at this site as early as 1228; it would have been located at the rear of today's pubs. By 1788, the old gaol had fallen into disrepair and needed replacement. George Moneypenny, one of England's leading prison designers, was instructed to create an appropriate façade. His work was known to be 'terrific' – as in filling onlookers with fright. Thus, it must have come as a surprise for the city councillors, who paid the substantial amount of £10,000 (£1.1 million in today's money), when Moneypenny delivered a neoclassical frontage of unexpected elegance. The symmetrical façade featured a central doorway flanked by evenly spaced windows, with the Governor's House at the centre. Rather than striking fear, this building evoked architectural awe! However, the building did not function as a prison for long. In 1846, a new county prison was built on Romsey Road, designed in the then fashionable 'panopticon' style: five wings radiating out from a central tower.

The old gaol on Jewry Street was bought by the council and reopened as one of the first free public libraries in the country in 1851. Later, it became an ironmonger, then a furniture shop, and finally opened as a pub in 1997. Stepping inside, the property's dark past won't escape you. You will find prison-inspired art scattered throughout the venue, a glass rack with a wire-and-chain effect and even a carpet patterned to echo prison bars.

Address The Old Gaolhouse, 11a Jewry Street, Winchester, SO23 8RZ | **Getting there** An 8-minute walk from Winchester railway station | **Hours** Sun–Thu 8am–midnight, Fri & Sat 8am–1am | **Tip** Want to know more about Winchester's criminal past? Winchester Tour Guides offer a guided walking tour on 'crime and punishment' (see www.visitwinchester.co.uk for details).

69__Oram's Arbour

Where the Romans didn't come first

As you reach the green open space that is Oram's Arbour – arriving via Clifton Terrace – the first feature that is likely to grab your attention is the memorial fountain at the edge of the park. With its pointed arches and ornate stonework, the Littlehales Monument is indeed intriguing to look at. Rooted and historic in demeanour, it might surprise you that this memorial was originally situated outside the Westgate. It was commissioned by Lancelot Littlehales to commemorate his mother Anne in 1880 but was moved to its current position 55 years later.

However, the true historical significance of this place is found in the ground. While it is commonly known that Winchester was an important Roman, Saxon and medieval town, this site helped to prove that Winchester was already well established during the Iron Age. The British archaeologist Christopher Hawkes first suggested the possibility of a pre-Roman settlement in 1930, but it took decades of excavations and analysis from the 1950s onwards to confirm this theory.

Today it is understood that Oram's Arbour once marked the western limit of an Iron Age *oppidum* that existed sometime between the 4th and the mid 1st centuries B.C. At Oram's Arbour, archaeologists uncovered a large ditch with an entrance typical of Iron Age fortifications. The ditch was around ten metres long and four metres deep and may have enclosed an area of around 20 hectares. Thus, university professor John Collis has argued, it would have been comparable in size to other Iron Age settlements in Wessex – like Maiden Castle or Hod Hill in Dorset.

Although today, with many layers of earth above it, the defences are no longer visible, if you amble across the tranquil, grassy park you can still feel the gentle rising that marks where the ramparts once stood.

Address Oram's Arbour, Clifton Road, Winchester, SO22 5BU | Getting there A 7-minute walk from Winchester railway station | Hours Accessible 24 hours | Tip Oram's Arbour is the ideal place for a picnic, but if you fancy food at the table, the delicious Pi Pizzas are just around the corner.

70_Owslebury

Walking with scarecrows

For one week in early summer, the picture-book village that is Owslebury becomes even more fairy-tale like. Then, it is not just the immaculately thatched roofs, the carefully tended lawns and the lush pink rosebushes that grab your attention but the impressively crafted scarecrows, too.

When the village team that organises the annual fundraiser came together in 2020 via Zoom to discuss their options, Siobhan Hand had no idea of the impact the project would have. 'We thought we might get a couple of people on the weekend.' Instead, their scarecrow trail has become a fixture during summer half term.

In their third year of participation, Owslebury residents Nicky and Jon Scott took on a particularly daring project. In their garden, you could spot the sturdy blue legs, broad red body and altogether wonderfully frightening appearance of Optimus Prime, the brave leader of the Autobots in the *Transformers* series. The Scotts dedicated more than four months to draw a draft, collect the necessary components, construct the frame and finally paint the robot in its vibrant colours. Tasked with creating a character starting with O, this children's character felt like the right amount of challenging.

The village is known for its creative spirit, and the windows of St Andrew's Church are said to have inspired the great painter Van Gogh, who, as a young artist, saw the designs for them in London. The windows were commissioned by William Carnegie, 8th Earl of Northesk, to commemorate his wife and daughter, and both windows depict the Virgin Mary. In one window, Mary is young and resembles William's daughter Lady Margaret; in the other she is older and reminiscent of William's wife Georgina, Countess of Northesk.

While the scarecrow trail is unique, the village's magic is worth experiencing any time of the year.

Address Main Road, Owslebury, Winchester, SO21 1LN | Getting there Take bus 63 to St Andrew's Church | Hours Accessible 24 hours | Tip Do not miss the culinary highlight that the gorgeous Restoration-era boutique country pub The Ship Inn has to offer.

71_P & G Wells

Britain's oldest bookshop (probably)

Winchester's full and vibrant history is perhaps layered most densely at 11 College Street. This charming bookshop – with dark wood panelling and the sweet, melancholic smell that lingers among shelves of printed paper – has not only served Winchester College for centuries but also counted great authors such as Charlotte Mary Yonge and Jane Austen, as well as poet John Keble, among its patrons.

While Hatchards, founded in 1797, claims to be London's oldest bookshop, the title of the oldest bookshop in *Britain* may in fact apply to P & G Wells. As current owner Steve Scholey shares, the earliest records of a bookseller and stationer in College Street date back to 1729. Initially located on the opposite side of College Street, the shop was moved first to No. 12 next door in 1757, then to its current location in 1789 by 'gentleman bookseller' John Burdon. That would have been the name associated with the bookshop when Jane Austen's father and her brother had accounts here. Although Jane Austen spent only the last weeks of her life in Winchester – at No. 8, just a few doors along – she knew the city well. Her eldest brother James attended Winchester College, and her father Reverend George Austen often visited the city on ecclesiastical business, to conduct his affairs or to buy books – some of which would be read by Jane.

At the back of the shop, in the historic bindery, you can still find the bespoke bookbinder's bench – believed to be the oldest in the country still in situ. Positioned against the back wall is a printing press from the 1720s, which was used to print the *Hampshire Chronicle* in the early 19th century. From the worn worktop of an 1860s guillotine (still fitted with a razor-sharp blade), Steve Scholey picks up a particular copy of James Boswell's *The Life of Samuel Johnson*. 'This is almost certainly,' he says, 'the very edition Jane Austen once had from this bookshop.'

Address P & G Wells, 11 College Street, Kingsgate Street, Winchester, SO23 9LZ | Getting there A 10-minute walk from Winchester bus station | Hours Mon–Sat 9am–5.30pm, Sun & Bank Holidays 11am–5pm | Tip Not just a reader but also a writer? The Hampshire Writer's Society offers engaging monthly talks and community spirit.

72 Paws for Thought

Cats and cappuccino

When Emma Blyth suddenly lost her beloved cat Louis in 2015, she wasn't prepared for the emptiness she would feel. To others, Louis might have been 'just' a cat, but to Emma, he was family. Any attempts to comfort her failed. It was during that time that Emma discovered the concept of cat cafés. And as she stepped over the threshold of one of them into the warm and welcoming space of kindness, gentle purrs and like-minded people, she knew she had found her calling.

In July 2018, she received the keys to a former children's clothing shop in Church Street, Romsey. The transformation began. Together with her soon-to-be husband, she stripped the walls bare and repainted them with soothing colours, filled the space with cosy sofas and tables for human guests, as well as climbing walls and snug corners for the feline residents. Four months later, without previous experience in hospitality, she opened her café Paws for Thought for coffee and cat lovers.

Just steps from the lively marketplace, the café greets you with the aroma of fresh coffee and buttery pastries. Despite its popularity, there is a serene calmness. The cappuccino arrives with cat-shaped chocolate powder on its foamy top and the signature 'Cats Got The Cream' Tea is served on a tray held aloft by a ceramic feline.

Eight cats call the café their home. They weave elegantly between tables, stretch out lazily on the warm windowsill or curl up in their little bunk beds. 'They're all rescues,' Emma says just as Kiara – the diva, according to the profile card placed on each table – jumps on her lap. Teddy, the naughty one – 'who has broken more cups than we can count' – saunters past. And Xena slips through a small cat flap in the fireplace, which leads to their private rest room.

In the midst of all this, Louis' legacy lives on. It was his shape and colour that inspired the café's sign.

Address Paws for Thought, 4 Church Street, Romsey, SO51 8BU | **Getting there** A 9-minute walk from Romsey railway station | **Hours** Mon, Thu, Fri & Sun 10am–4pm, Sat 10am–5.15pm | **Tip** The best day to visit Romsey is on a Sunday, when the Romsey Makers Market takes place from 10am to 3pm at the Cornmarket.

73__The Railway Inn

The journey of great music

Great music is like a train journey. It carries you to new places and while its destination might be exciting or sad or dark, its regular rhythm comforts you along the way. Thus, it seems only fitting that Winchester's most iconic music venue is situated in a pub once used as a local for railway workers.

The Railway Inn, comfortably positioned on the steep St Paul's Hill behind Winchester railway station, has hosted numerous great artists in the last five decades. Singer-songwriters Ed Sheeran and Dua Lipa have stood on its stage; Mumford & Sons have performed, as has Imelda May; PJ Harvey played on her acoustic guitar, and actor Colin Firth and Coldplay's Will Champion – both students at Peter Symonds College – might even have dropped in for a drink or two with their fellow students.

That the music venue still exists today is thanks to one particularly loyal local. Dan Lloyd has been a regular since he visited the music pub to watch a friend's band in the late 1990s. 'It had the right sort of vibe, a welcoming atmosphere. The people were nicer; the bar staff were kind.' So, when he heard that the venue was to be closed in the summer of 2014, he was distraught but didn't hesitate. Two months later, he opened its front doors as its new owner. 'The first years were chaos,' Dan Lloyd admits. 'There was so much to be done.' The place needed fitting out, repainting, the electrics redone... And yet when, during a gig, the pub is so packed that the crowd seems to morph into one entity and the beat reverberates through its walls; when new guests become regulars and new events series become beloved fixtures – there is nothing he would rather be doing.

In a way, running a music pub is like a train journey, too. Naturally, the destination is the making of a profit, but the real reason you are on board is the vibe.

Address The Railway Inn, 3 St Paul's Hill, SO22 5AE | Getting there A 5-minute walk from Winchester railway station | Hours Mon–Thu 5pm–midnight, Fr 5pm–2am, Sat noon–1am, Sun noon–midnight | Tip A fan of live music? There are also great gigs at O'Neill's Winchester and The Dove Inn in Micheldever.

74 Regimental Garden

Finding peace among peacekeepers

With its elegant red brick front, its symmetrical structure and high windows overlooking a neatly trimmed lawn, Serle's House is sure to catch your eye as you pass Southgate Street. Originally, Sir Christopher Wren had proposed the area between Winchester Castle and Southgate Street as a palace for King Charles II. After a period when the monarchy had little use for the city, he was rather fond of Winchester. But after Wren's death in 1723, the plan quickly fell through. Instead, William Sheldon purchased the site in 1730 to build his family home. Half a century later, it came into the possession of James Serle, whose son forged ties with the military that persist to this day.

While most of Winchester's military museums (such as those of the HorsePower, Gurkha or Rifleman's Museum) focus on national collections, Serle's House is home to the Royal Hampshire Regiment's Museum. This regiment served the British from 1702 – when it was formed by Meredith's Regiment – until 1992, when it amalgamated with the Queen's Regiment to become the Princess of Wales's Royal Regiment. Thus, despite offering a regional military collection, this museum might be the most emotionally resonant for Wintonians. Every serving member of the regiment's first battalion who went to war in 1914 is listed in an elegant wooden frame surrounding the battalion's banner.

One of the museum's most serene spots can be found outside. To the left of Serle's House, under the sprawling canopy of a yew tree and at the corner of a green flower border, lies a rounded wooden bench, inviting you to pause and relax. Although the estate is situated on the busy Southgate Street, the shield of leafy greenery around the little nook exudes a sense of peace. This is fitting, as among the flowers surrounding Serle's House the ashes of former soldiers are scattered, finding peace next to peacekeepers.

Address Serle's House, Southgate Street, SO23 9EG | **Getting there** An 11-minute walk from Winchester railway station | **Hours** Tue–Fri 10am–4pm, Sat & Bank Holidays 10.30am–3pm | **Tip** There is one more military museum just outside the city – The Royal Logistics Corps Museum in Worthy Down.

75 Rick Stein

Sublime seafood's Winchester edition

While exotic ingredients and extravagant produce might be quick to dazzle one's taste buds, real culinary excellence shows itself in simplicity: if a humble pasta manages to wow you, then you have found true talent. In the case of Cornish celebrity chef Rick Stein, the weapon of choice is, of course, seafood: smoky sea bream, golden battered Cornish mackerel, buttery prawns. 'Nothing,' he once said, 'is more exhilarating than fresh fish simply cooked.' (Although, potentially, cooking turbot hollandaise for Queen Elizabeth II might have been.)

In 1975, the British chef, cookbook author and TV presenter opened his first restaurant The Seafood in the picturesque port village of Padstow with his then wife, the interior designer Jill Stein. Since then, his venture has grown to include ten restaurants and forty hotel rooms, four shops as well as a cookery school. For more than a decade, he has also brought 'the taste of Cornwall' to Winchester. In 2014, he opened his first restaurant outside of the west country in Winchester's High Street, offering fresh Cornish catches as well as coffee mornings to support local businesses.

In a brightly modern yet comfortable, grounded atmosphere, he offers rich shellfish ragout with tender meat and an aromatic sauce, or fresh sashimi of sea bream, or salmon served with spicy wasabi, as well as – in a more unusual combination – freshly opened Dorset oysters paired with a spicy sausage. Rick advises taking a bite of each in turn, followed by a sip of cold, refreshing wine (well, if he insists…).

Finally, do not miss the dessert that celebrates this city: the Winchester Pudding. Based on a recipe from 1906, this steamed sponge pudding is enriched with orange, sultanas and currants, flavoured with the sharp tang of Grand Marnier, soothing butterscotch sauce and mild Cornish clotted cream. Simple, yet refined.

Address Rick Stein, 8 High Street, Winchester, SO23 9JX | Getting there A short walk from Winchester bus station | Hours Wed & Thu noon–3pm & 5–8.30pm, Fri & Sat noon–9pm, Sun noon–3pm | Tip If you like fresh fish, try the produce of Johnson's Fish, a family-run seafood business, which sells on Wednesdays from Cobbs Farm Shop.

76 The Riddle of Curle's Passage

To pray or not to pray

In 1632, Bishop Walter Curle reached breaking point. The tranquillity of Winchester Cathedral, essential for reflection and prayer, was constantly being disturbed by people using the sacred space as a shortcut from the city to the green spaces. Frustrated by this intrusion, Bishop Walter Curle commissioned the creation of a passageway, to redirect foot traffic away from the cathedral's interior. To achieve this, arches were cut into the flying buttresses on the right of the cathedral, creating what is now known as The Slype or Curle's Passage.

Almost 400 years later, the legacy of Curle's solution is still apparent on the cathedral's exterior walls. If you look closely, on the right side of the grand Cathedral gate, slightly above eye level, you will see a carving of two hands pointing in opposite directions. Accompanying these hands are Latin inscriptions that read *Illac precator hac viator ambula*. Translated, this means 'Walk that way to pray, this way to pass through'. In the 17th century, Latin was primarily spoken by scholars and clergy, so the Latin carving adds a layer of historical intrigue, presenting what has become known as the 'Curle's Passageway Riddle'.

In the spring of 2023, the passage found itself in the limelight once more. Giant headlights were positioned on cherry pickers, shining their bright light through the church windows to simulate sunlight for the filming of the Netflix show *The Crown*. Winchester Cathedral stood in for both St Paul's Cathedral and Westminster Abbey – including a dramatic depiction of Princess Diana's funeral during the sixth and final season. As curious onlookers slowed their pace to catch a glimpse of the filming, it was amusing to think that for the first time, some might have wished for the passageway's removal, longing for a route through the cathedral once more.

Address 9 The Close, Winchester, SO23 9LS | Getting there A 9-minute walk from Winchester railway station | Hours Accessible 24 hours | Tip The passage and its surrounding area are particularly stunning at Christmas time.

77_The Rifleman's Museum

Giants of the past made miniature

No Western battle has been so immortalised in art, public infrastructure and the cultural heritage as the Duke of Wellington's final victory over Napoleon Bonaparte on 18 June 1815: the Battle of Waterloo. It appears in Thackeray's *Vanity Fair*, Victor Hugo's *Les Misérables* and Sir Arthur Conan Doyle's *The Great Shadow*. It lent its name to a Tube station as well as a bridge in the English capital, became an idiom and even inspired the Swedish pop band ABBA to the song that would win them the Eurovision Song Contest in Brighton in 1974. And few places in southern England remember it as vividly as Winchester.

As you enter the first floor of Winchester's Rifleman's Museum in the Peninsula Barracks, you are greeted by an impressive model diorama of the historic battle. This diorama is not just the centrepiece of the military museum but also one of the largest models in the country. Occupying around 30 square metres, it contains more than 31,000 model soldiers and horses. The model concentrates not on one single moment but rather depicts a fluid vision of the entire battle. In a captivating sound and light commentary, journalist Kate Adie takes visitors through the key moments of the battle, bringing the day to life in a unique way.

Two of the Rifleman's preceding regiments – the 52nd Light Infantry and the 95th Rifles – played a vital part in the Battle of Waterloo. Both regiments were awarded with the battle honour 'Waterloo'. In 1989, the Royal Green Jackets Museum (which became the Rifleman's Museum in 2025) unveiled the diorama that had been created by Mike Buxton of Valhalla Models. Look closely and the model reveals not only fierce scenes of conflict but also lighthearted moments: a gardener protecting his cabbage patch, sergeants carrying canteens with the gin rations they drank themselves or, as a little maker's prank, a British soldier laughing as he passes water against a tree.

Address The Rifleman's Museum, Peninsula Barracks, Romsey Road, SO23 8TS | Getting there A 10-minute walk from Winchester railway station | Hours Mon–Sat 10am–4pm | Tip The other military museums at the historic Peninsula Barracks are also well worth a visit.

78 Romsey Abbey

The tomb of Lord Mountbatten

Standing in the middle of the nave and facing the imposing chancel, the grandeur of this ecclesiastical building does not escape your notice. But then, Romsey Abbey, 13 miles southwest of Winchester Cathedral, is the biggest and one of the earliest established parish churches in Hampshire. As early as 907, a nunnery had been erected, and tales of the inhabitants' curious reputations are still told to this day.

The first abbess, Merwinna (granddaughter of Alfred the Great and half-sister of St Edburga) is said to have recited psalms standing completely naked in the River Test at night as an act of sanctity. Another abbess, a couple of hundred years later, allegedly kept a monkey. Indeed, the nuns were repeatedly told off by the Bishop of Winchester for their 'unruly behaviour', shares Head Verger Christopher Harpham as he walks through the abbey, past the stepping stone dedicated to the three Johns and one Robert who managed to raise enough funds to buy the church from Henry VIII, past St Anne's Chapel – which displays the low-relief carving of a Crucifixion believed to be the oldest rood in the country – to St Nicholas Chapel, where you find the black headstone set in the ground that is the main reason people visit the abbey to this day.

The stone reads *Admiral of the Fleet Earl Mountbatten of Burma* and marks the burial place of the great-uncle of King Charles III. Earl Mountbatten was assassinated off the coast of Mullaghmore Peninsula in County Sligo, Ireland, by the Irish Republican Army on 27 August 1979. And while his state funeral on 5 September took place in Westminster Abbey, he was laid to rest here as the Mountbatten family inhabits Broadlands Estate near Romsey.

Contrary to tradition, the grave is not aligned on an east-west line but positioned north-south in order for him to face towards Portsmouth – in the direction of the sea – where the ashes of his wife, Edwina, were scattered.

Address Romsey Abbey, Church Lane, Romsey, SO51 8EP | Getting there Take bus 66 to Romsey, then a 5-minute walk | Hours Mon–Fri 10.30am–4.30pm, Sun 11am–5pm | Tip If you feel peckish after the visit at the abbey, The White Horse on Market Place does wonderful meals.

79_Royal Oak

Where England's twice-crowned queen resided

When it comes to pubs, age is often a hallmark of quality and charm. As a result, many establishments across the country have laid claim to being the oldest one in England. While many of their true origins may be lost to history, the Royal Oak in Winchester stands as a worthy contender. This traditional pub is entered through a quaint, rustic entrance in a particularly narrow side street. After taking the staircase to the left side of the bar to a lower seating area, you are greeted by a display showcasing the original foundations. This flint construction allegedly dates back to the beginning of the last millennium, when King Æthelred gave this property – together with the surrounding city, really – as a wedding present to his wife, Queen Emma (who later became wife of King Cnut, which made her the only ever twice-crowned Queen of England).

The pub's name, however, is rooted in another royal connection. During the English Civil War in the 1600s – the pub likes to share – it became a gathering place for those opposed to Oliver Cromwell. The royal supporters discreetly wore an oak leaf to show their allegiance to the monarchy. But after Charles II famously hid in an English oak at Boscobel House in Shropshire to escape the Roundheads, hundreds of pubs throughout the country were given this name. What lends this Royal Oak unusual credibility is its proximity to royal history: after the Restoration, King Charles II chose to build a new royal residence on the site of Winchester Castle. The nearby pub is believed to have been named in tribute to his legacy.

Today, it is a favourite haunt of students, who indulge in fish and chips and cider while revelling in the ghostly stories that surround the premises. But do the drinks really slide off tables 3 and 9, and do the menu boxes actually move across the table…? You will have to visit and judge for yourself.

Address Royal Oak, Royal Oak Passage, Winchester, SO23 9AU | Getting there A 10-minute walk from Winchester railway station | Hours Mon–Wed noon–11pm, Thu noon–midnight, Fri & Sat 11–12.30am, Sun noon–10pm | Tip If you enjoy haunted pubs, do not miss the red room in the Eclipse Inn.

80_ The Sarsen Stones of Twyford

Where druids (possibly) mingled

If you think Twyford, a quiet Hampshire village, and Stonehenge, southwest England's busiest tourist attraction, can't possibly have anything in common – think again. Specifically, keep your eyes on the left side as you follow Berry Lane in Twyford towards Berry Bridge. Just a couple of steps past the end of the graveyard, slightly hidden under nettles and ivy, you will see the smooth surface of a surprisingly large stone. This is the same type used in the Stonehenge monument – a sarsen stone. Found regularly in southern England, sarsen stones occur naturally in chalky landscape. Due to their size and random appearance, they have always carried an air of mystique and are thought to have been used by druids for religious practices, often arranged to construct awe-inspiring monuments. At Stonehenge, sarsen stones make up the large, dark grey boulders, standing upright and sometimes laid on top of two upright ones. To druids, circles symbolised eternity as well as the cycle of nature; together with a well and a yew or oak tree such a space became a sacred temple in which to conduct their practice.

While the slightly buried sarsen stone on Berry Lane seems oddly scattered in the countryside, it is linked to a possible druidical temple nearby: 12 sarsen stones neatly arranged in a circle, believed to originate in the Bronze Age. Sadly, you cannot see them today as the tower of St Mary Church has been built on top.

The Victorian edifice itself is worth a visit too. Built in 1876, it replaced a former Saxon church. Its alternating bands of neat stonework, where lighter and darker stones alternate in horizontal lines, creates a striking striped effect that is reminiscent of London's Natural History Museum. Indeed, the church was designed by the same architect, Alfred Waterhouse.

Address Berry Lane, Twyford, SO21 1NT | Getting there Take bus 69 to Northfields, then a 4-minute walk | Hours Accessible 24 hours | Tip From enigmatic to engineering: when in Twyford, don't miss the preserved Edwardian water pumping station, which is now the Waterworks Museum.

81 The Sewage Lamp

Joseph Webb's obscure olfactory idea

In a slight bend of Great Minster Street, wedged between the Minster Gallery and Cathedral Green, and thus easily overlooked, stands an innovative – albeit slightly stomach-turning – example of Victorian ingenuity. This black streetlamp is Winchester's last remaining sewer gas destructor lamp. The two bars on either side were once used to rest a ladder on when the lamp was lit each evening.

The Birmingham-based inventor Joseph Edmund Webb patented this design on 21 May 1895. He hoped his lamp would not only be used for 'street or other lighting purposes' but also 'extract the obnoxious gases and vapour collected or generated from a sewer' and 'destroy all germs and noxious qualities prior to their passing into the atmosphere'. After the disaster of the Big Stink in the summer of 1858, when the combination of hot weather and untreated waste made life unbearable in London, solutions for sanitation were in high demand. Webb's invention was partly rooted in the now-abandoned miasma theory. According to this theory, epidemics spread when people breathe in the 'bad air' of rotten, organic matter. And although Webb was aware of bacteria, he evidently still believed those to linger in the sewer gas. To address this, he proposed sterilising the gas by raising it to 700 degrees Celsius.

Webb's gas destructor lanterns became particularly popular in hilly towns, where gas tended to build up in pockets – like Sheffield, which received 84 such lamp posts. The sewage lamps were also popular in high-rise urban areas like Carting Lane in London, where the so-called 'stink pipes' (a sort of chimney for sewage gas to drift off) could not be implemented. And, lastly, they were installed in cathedral cities like Ripon, Durham and Winchester. By 1878, 41 of these lamps had been introduced in Hampshire's capital. Today, only the one remains.

Address Loverose Way, Winchester, SO23 9EP | Getting there A 12-minute walk from Winchester railway station | Hours Accessible 24 hours | Tip During a longer stroll around the cathedral grounds, the nearby food truck on Market Street offers lovely coffee to energise you.

82 Sir Harold Hillier Gardens

Learning from Chelsea, rivalling Kew

On average, the British monarch awards about 2,000 honours and 80 knighthoods or damehoods each year. However, since the beginning of the 20th century, only two people are believed to have been knighted for their services to ornamental horticulture. One was Sir Harry Veitch, who established the Chelsea Flower Show. The other was a garden enthusiast who succeeded in creating one of the largest collections of hardy trees and shrubs in the world. Harold Hillier, whose grandfather had trained at Veitch's nursery and later opened his own nursery at 80 High Street in Winchester, was born with a passion for plants. Yet, he aspired to do more than simply continue the family nursery. On 3 June 1953, a day after Queen Elizabeth II's Coronation, he and his family moved into Jermyn's House near Romsey, a stately home with 41 surrounding acres of land.

Today, Sir Harold Hillier Gardens house 40,000 individual plants and 600 Champion Trees – record-holding examples in height or girth or both (by comparison, Kew Gardens has 300 such specimens). Among these is a striking *Picea orientalis* 'Skylands', with golden-yellow needle tips and dark green undersides, giving it the appearance of being sun-drenched. Another standout is the 'Metasequoia', or Dawn Redwood, whose leaf features on the garden's logo. The gardens boast an area that shines in each season. Yet, the most iconic area is Magnolia Avenue in front of Jermyn's House. The idea came from Hillier's friend Lord Savile, who, during a visit, looked out of his bedroom window and envisioned rows of gnarly trees adorned with soft-pink blossoms. Harold Hillier was easily convinced: 'I for one take pleasure and satisfaction in planting an 18-inch-high tree magnolia, which though I can never see it flower, I can even now enjoy its invisible colour and latent fragrance.' A humility from which many could learn.

Address Sir Harold Hillier Gardens, Jermyns Lane, Ampfield, Romsey, SO51 0QA | **Getting there** Take bus 66 to Hillier Arboretum, then a 10-minute walk | **Hours** Check website for seasonal opening hours (www.hants.gov.uk/thingstodo/hilliergardens/visit/opening-times) | **Tip** For a lovely dinner after your walk around the garden, visit the Dog and Crook pub just a few minutes away.

83 Sound II

A sculpture deep in reflection

Crypts love to whisper of secrets, leaving you with titillating goosebumps of anticipation. However, the crypt in Winchester Cathedral will also make you gasp with surprise, thanks to the donation of Sir Anthony Gormley.

In the early 1990s, the British artist visited the cathedral. A graduate of The Central School of Art and Design, Goldsmiths College and The Slade School of Fine Art, Anthony Gormley developed a fascination for urban construction and working with industrial materials. He became particularly interested in the relationship between architecture and the human body, often using his own body as the subject of his work. In an unusual process, he is covered in a film of plastic, using small tubes in his nose to breathe as the plastic solidifies. These moulds are then used to create a sculpture made of roofing lead and fibreglass.

Entering the crypt, Gormley announced that he had 'a piece of sculpture that would look magical in this place'. He donated his sculpture *Sound II* and requested its exact position on the clay and lime floor, where it has been standing since 1993. In the dim light of the Norman groin vaulting, a tall standing statue has its hands cupped at chest level, as if cradling a bowl with water. Its head is bent as if studying its own reflection in the mirror, invoking the idea of contemplation. True magic happens when the crypt floods, which happens regularly as the cathedral is built on the soft soil of a riverbed. Then, the hollow figure fills with water that runs through a hole in its solar plexus into the bowl of its hands, and the surrounding water adds another layer of reflection.

These days, there is also a different interpretation: the statue of a man focusing on something in his cupped hands amidst a stunning space has an odd resemblance to people staring at their smartphones – even in the most beautiful surroundings.

Address The Crypt, Winchester Cathedral, 9 The Close, SO23 9LS, www.winchester-cathedral.org.uk | Getting there A 7-minute walk from Winchester bus station | Hours Mon–Sat 9am–5pm, Sun 12.30–3pm; check website for crypt tour times | Tip Keen to see more art? The Minster Gallery, facing the cathedral, shows paintings and sculpture by contemporary British and international artists.

84_South Downs Social

Made for cyclists, enjoyed by everyone

Our passions have a curious tendency to circle back to us. Growing up in Ireland, Neil Wyatt loved nothing more than cycling up the Wicklow Mountains, pretending to be one of his heroes, Sean Kelly or Stephen Roche. But as the distractions of teenage years set in, he stopped riding, turning to other interests: art and music. He moved to England, went to university and began working as an events promoter for the BBC. It wasn't until his late twenties, when he hired a bike to cycle around the Ring of Kerry, that his passion reignited and a vision began to form: a bustling cycling café with a little mezzanine studio and a big TV showing the Tour de France.

As a hobby, he and his wife started a small project, The Handmade Cyclist, designing apparel and prints for bike enthusiasts. But then the pandemic hit and within 48 hours, Neil lost all his work. The solution? To focus on their hobby, their vision. In December 2021, he opened a pop-up shop in Kings Walk. Four years later, it has grown into a hybrid café so popular that Neil had to add extra seats on the first floor. The café serves smooth coffee, hearty breakfasts and loaded sandwiches in a relaxed atmosphere beneath a canopy of signed cycling jerseys. Visitors can find stylish cycle wear and thrilling cycle reads, cookbooks by The Cycling Chef and even Winchester-made peanut butter intended to fuel the next adventure. It also hosts cycling talks and is a meeting point for cycling clubs – though you shouldn't hesitate to step in, even if you are not a bike lover.

'If someone had told me 10 years ago I'd be running a café,' Neil says, 'I wouldn't have believed it.' Yet here it is: the bustling café, the mezzanine studio, the big screen. Only one thing is missing, Neil laughs. 'I am so busy, I never have time to watch the Tour de France.' But it is a sacrifice he is happy to make.

Address The South Downs Social, 3–4 Kings Walk, SO23 8AF | **Getting there** A 4-minute walk from Winchester bus station | **Hours** Mon–Fri 9am–5pm, Sat 8.30am–5pm, Sun 9am–4pm | **Tip** This is for cycling and history lovers: King Alfred's Way is a 217-mile cycle loop around historic Wessex, which starts and ends in Winchester.

85__South Downs Sourdough

You will loaf how easy breadmaking is

With the crust cracking soothingly beneath the bread knife, a little bit of butter is spread onto the still-warm slice. Then, a delicious first bite. All that was needed was local bread flour and water. Can it really be this simple?

Few culinary products have risen – literally as well as metaphorically – to such fame in recent years as sourdough. In a collective desire for deeper connection with one's food and better gut health, more and more people turned to home baking. But as tips and recipes were shared in detailed videos or dedicated blog posts, breadmaking evolved into a complex, ritualised art form, a process so revered that many shied away from even attempting a simple sourdough starter. It is this notion Mark Horner seeks to challenge.

A trained management consultant, Mark began exploring breadmaking when his children were young. 'I wanted to understand the process. And I didn't want to give them lots of sugar,' he says. Initially, he worked with dried yeast and a bread machine, but 18 years ago he decided to give sourdough a go. 'And I've never looked back,' he smiles.

In 2018, he opened his artisan bakery school at The Brick House, a charming country home in Cheriton, tucked in the South Downs National Park. In his countryside kitchen, overlooking a neatly trimmed English lawn, he calmly explains each step: starter, fermentation, preservation. Focused, the small group of participants nod, take notes and carefully add the correct measure of ingredients into the bowls before them. Over the course of the day, tentative smiles appear – when the dough becomes denser, when it rises and once more when the dough is tipped from the banneton onto the baking tray. But all of that is topped at 5 o'clock when the comforting smell of warm bread fills the kitchen and the students pull the hot trays out of the oven. Resting on top: six perfect, deep brown, wonderfully crusty loaves. 'Wow!' the participants gasp, it really was that simple.

Address South Downs Sourdough, The Brick House, Cheriton, SO24 0PR, www.southdownssourdough.co.uk | Getting there A 7-minute walk from Winchester bus station | Hours See website for schedule of classes (advance booking required) | Tip Before you leave Cheriton, stop at the cosy country pub The Flower Pots Inn, which offers beers from its own brewery.

86 St Giles Hill

A spectacle for the senses

For the best view of the city, turn away from it. Walk south on the High Street, past the statue of King Alfred, cross St Swithun's Bridge and continue along Bridge Street. Go straight on at the roundabout, past The Rising Sun, and turn right onto the footpath at the bend of the road. Climb the 149 steps up the hill until you reach a little park. Turn right and walk along the edge of the park until you meet a little platform. Marvel at the picturesque city that spreads out below you.

Chances are, it will be quiet in the hilltop park when you visit it. Yet during the Middle Ages, this space would host a spectacle so great that it attracted visitors from across the English Channel. In 1096, King William II granted Bishop Walkelin of Winchester the right to hold a fair on St Giles Hill in the last days of August (as 1 September was St Giles Day). 'The medieval bishops of Winchester were not just a bit rich,' says Winchester city guide Lorraine Estelle, 'they were incredibly wealthy.' And they were keen to increase their wealth. During the fair, no merchant in a 35-kilometre radius was allowed to 'sell, buy or set out for sale any merchandise in any place other than the fair under penalty of forfeiture of goods to the Bishop'. Despite these rules – or maybe because of them – the fair was a grand success. The stalls were strictly organised by theme and traders came not only from England but also from Spain, France and Italy. Soon the feast was extended from its original three days to sixteen. The atmosphere was electric: 'There were lemurs, apes and songbirds, fortune tellers, dancers – and possibly pickpockets,' says Lorraine.

Yet it was not destined to last. Interest started to wane at the end of the 12th century and the fair stopped completely in 1420. However, in 1975 the spirit of the festival returned – by means of the Winchester Hat Fair.

Address The Viewpoint, St Giles Hill, Winchester, SO23 8BL | Getting there A 19-minute walk from Winchester bus station | Hours Accessible 24 hours | Tip Why not make a little detour to St Giles Hill Graveyard, with graves dating back more than 300 years?

87 St Swithun-upon-Kingsgate

Psalms and snuffling above the city gate

Dozens of churches are dedicated to the well-loved Saxon saint St Swithun. Yet one of them arguably has the strongest claim to this title – being located in the very city where he worked as bishop in the 9th century. But St Swithun-upon-Kingsgate is unusual for another reason: this church is built directly into the fabric of Winchester's ancient city walls. To reach it, you must enter by an old wooden gate and climb a narrow stone staircase. The church consists of a single 'upper room' and while its interior might be simple – white-washed walls, unadorned wooden beams and a small altar – as you sit down in one of the wooden pews, you are cocooned by a soothing calm.

The church has existed since at least 1264, when the *Annales Monasterii de Wintonia* records a revolt, where houses were burned, and among those 'Kingsgate with the Church of Saint Swithun above' (*Kingate cum ecclesia Sancti Swythuni supra*). It was not unusual for a medieval church to be situated atop a city gate, as it gave travellers room to pray after a treacherous journey, yet St Swithun is believed to be the only one in England still in use.

The chapel has also enjoyed literary fame. In 1855, Anthony Trollope (who attended Winchester College) published *The Warden* – the first book in his *Chronicle of Barsetshire* series – a novel centring around questions of ethics, duty and reform within the Anglican church. In this novel, St Cuthbert's Church is portrayed as an established Anglican church within the fictional cathedral town of Barchester (the last seven letters give a clue), frequented by Reverend Septimus Harding, the warden of nearby Hiram's Hospital (Hospital of St Cross springs to mind).

However, the church's most unusual anecdote comes from the 17th century, when the gate porter, Robert Allen, and his wife lived in the church – and shared this space with their pigs.

Address St Swithun-upon-Kingsgate, Kingsgate Street, Winchester, SO23 9PD | **Getting there** A 9-minute walk from Winchester bus station | **Hours** Daily noon–4pm; service Sun 6pm | **Tip** You can see the modern shrine remembering the 9th century bishop when you visit Winchester Cathedral.

88 St Swithun's Bridge

Where it shall rain for 40 days

You have probably heard of the celestial power attributed to St Swithun: his ability to bring 40 days of rain if it rains on his feast day. You might even be aware that the day in question is 15 July. But did you know that the origin of the weather proverb – 'St Swithun's day, if thou be fair, / For forty days it will remain. / St Swithun's Day, if thou bring rain, / For forty days it will remain' – can be traced back to the heart of Winchester?

Swithun (or Swithin), born around A.D. 800, was an Anglo-Saxon Bishop of Winchester. He is said to have been a wise and kind bishop, secretly repairing churches at night and building a stone bridge across the River Itchen to make it easier for poor people to sell their wares. While the current stone bridge at the junction of High Street and Bridge Street was built in 1813 by George Forder, the inscription on the central pier remembers its predecessor.

In keeping with his humility, Swithun asked to be buried outside 'where passers-by should pass over his grave and raindrops from the eaves drop upon it'. When he died in 862, he was laid to rest outside the northern wall of Old Minster. However, on 15 July 971, his remains were moved from their original resting place in the churchyard to a shrine inside the cathedral. As legend has it, a great storm ensued – lasting for no less than 40 days and 40 nights. A divine sign of his displeasure?

Many miracles are said to have taken place after his death. Indeed, so many that the monks, who were instructed to go to church every time one occurred, sometimes had to get up three to four times a night. However, only one miracle was recorded during his lifetime, and it is associated with his stone bridge: a market woman, while crossing it, dropped her basket of eggs and they all broke. As she burst into a pitiful cry, St Swithun rushed by and returned the eggs to her – unbroken.

Address City Bridge, Bridge Street, Winchester, SO23 9BH | Getting there A short walk from Winchester bus station | Hours Accessible 24 hours | Tip Let time drift by, in this lovely spot next to the bridge: the terrace garden of The Bishop on the Bridge.

89_Theatre Royal Winchester

The ghost of John Simpkins

Theatre, in general, sits in the liminal space between the real and the imagined; it likes to play with expectations. In this, Theatre Royal Winchester succeeds at first glance. Stepping through the glass door of the sleek building and passing the modern bar, one cannot help but be surprised when entering the auditorium: a heritage, Edwardian-style theatre. It is, Chief Executive Deryck Newland explains, one of the best surviving examples of cine-variety theatres. At the time of World War I, before public broadcasting, people depended on these venues to receive news from the front and sometimes enjoyed a silent film. As projectors used to get very hot back then, little variety acts were presented while the bulbs cooled down.

These days, the theatre presents well over 300 performances a year, ranging from dance, drama and stand-up comedy to tribute bands. Almost a quarter of the total annual audience come to watch one of their 60 panto performances in the six weeks leading up to Christmas.

Long before the red curtain was regularly raised, curtains with more subdued colours would have been drawn nightly. Winchester's theatre venue was once a hotel. This comes with its quirks: little offices that used to be toilets; lots of little steps up and down, as the hotel made use of all the available space; and – the ghost. One of the two brothers who built the theatre, John Simpkins is believed to still haunt the house. He has been spotted coming out of the wall on the left side of the auditorium. Making his way along row A, he pauses, maybe looking for his initial, and disappointedly marches on to disappear into the wall on the right-hand side. When paranormal experts explored the place, they indeed measured the highest level of activity at the spot where John's spirit is said to disappear. It is a story eagerly retold. The best stories sit in the liminal space between the real and the imagined.

Address Theatre Royal Winchester, Jewry Street, SO23 8SB, www.theatreroyalwinchester.co.uk | Getting there A 4-minute walk from Winchester railway station | Hours Box office Tue–Sat 10am–1pm; bar opens two hours before the shows; see website for behind-the-scenes tours and show details | Tip Looking for a glass of wine after the theatre performance? Stop at the magnificent Margaux Lounge just a couple of hundred yards away on Jewry Street.

90__Tillius

Winchester's cabinet of curiosities

Meet Roxy the Rabbit, a devoted cucumber lover who could devour an entire cucumber and lived to a ripe old age. Then, there are the mice – Basil, Sage and Thyme – who were sadly killed by a cat. Pepper, who met an untimely end on the road. And, of course, Birch. The house mouse perched on a little desk, reimagined as the backyard purveyor of dodgy snail serum.

'We are a bit like Marmite,' Barnaby admits, as he steps into what is likely Winchester's most peculiar shop. 'You either love us or hate us.' Eccentricity, he continues, runs in the family – they had always lived in a very maximalist world, collected the unusual and curated their homes like no other. The idea for their business took root when Barnaby, a former marine biologist seeking a more practical career, joined forces with his mother, who had experience in interior design, and his father, who was eager to take part.

In 2019, they opened their first cabinet of curiosities in their hometown Tavistock, Devon. But a few years later, Winchester called them. While wandering through the city in search of a new space, Barnaby recalls his mother leaning against an old hair and beauty salon and declaring, 'I think this is it'. A year later, the family had transformed the space – painting the walls black (a far more exhausting task than they had anticipated), adding gilded features, arranging eclectic décor as well as extravagant accessories, and creating – tucked away at the back – the most mysterious and fascinating room.

Beyond indulgent candles, opulent tableware, fine jewellery and delicate flowers, the shop offers something far rarer: taxidermy. With meticulous craftsmanship, artists prepare and arrange animals – each having died from natural causes or accidents – into intricate, artistic arrangements. In a world where death is often still a taboo, Tillius seeks to celebrate it.

Address Tillius, 63 High Street, Winchester, SO23 9BX | **Getting there** A 9-minute walk from Winchester railway station | **Hours** Mon–Thu 10am–5pm, Fri & Sat 10am–5.30pm, Sun 11am–4.30pm | **Tip** If you are fascinated by taxidermy, Haslemere Educational Museum, one hour east of Winchester, offers one of the largest natural history museums in central southern England with over 240,000 specimens.

91_Victorian Letter Box

Spreading the words by the millions

The Victorian era was marked by groundbreaking firsts. In 1837, the British inventors Sir Charles Wheatstone and Sir William Fothergill Cooke publicly demonstrated a successful telegraph, sent from Euston and received at Camden station, and thus changing the speed of communication forever. In 1847, the Scottish doctor James Young Simpson became the first obstetrician to use chloroform as anaesthetic on a human, revolutionising the field of medicine. And in 1851, the first World's Fair took place at the Crystal Palace in London, sparking a wave of landmarks like the Eiffel Tower, the Seattle's Space Needle and the Atomium in Brussels.

Yet, one seemingly small invention may have had the biggest impact on everyday life. On 2 May 1840, four days before its official release, the first ever Penny Black was affixed to a letter in Bath and sent on its way to London. Prior to that, sending letters was an expensive and complicated endeavour. It had been the recipient's responsibility to pay. Thus, if they refused, the letter might have been sent back or destroyed. Additionally, there was no standard rate. To illustrate the effect of the reform: in 1839 only 76 million letters had been sent; by 1850 this number had risen to 350 million.

In Winchester, two letterboxes from that era are still in use. The more ordinary one can be found on Sleeper's Hill, while the more unusual one is located in Kingsgate Street. 'It is a Ludlow type, named after the designer James Ludlow, not the town,' explains Andrew R Young, chair of the British Letterbox Study Group. Made from wood with an iron and enamel facia, they first appeared in 1885 and were usually inserted into the front of a sub-post office, 'as this one was,' Andrew adds, 'and openable from the rear.' This way collections could be made without going outside – a particularly useful feature during the generally colder Victorian winters.

Address Kingsgate Street on the corner of College Street, Winchester, SO23 9PE | Getting there An 11-minute walk from Winchester bus station | Hours Accessible 24 hours | Tip The little Cornflower Gift Shop just next to the letterbox is a haven for charming accessories.

92 The Water Garden

The perfect soil: stirred not shaken

If you turn into the alleyway just before Colebrook Street, you cannot help but notice the little water garden to your right: a spring-fed pond framed by dark green hedges and gnarly magnolia trees. The perfect symmetry of its arrangement, and the subtle yet elegant design, suggest its creator might have been an experienced landscape architect, a passionate designer or skilful artist. However, the previous profession of Sir Peter Smithers, the Conservative MP who managed to block the creation of a gas reservoir underneath the cathedral city and who bought the stretch of land in Colebrook Street in 1958 to offer passers-by a new view of the church, was slightly more exciting.

During World War II, Peter Smithers was recruited as a spy by MI6. In this role, he 'organised the last-minute escape of British refugees as the Nazis advanced through France,' 'captured German spies landing in England' and then, as a charming naval attaché, 'spread disinformation in the diplomatic set in wartime Washington,' the *Financial Times* summarised in his obituary in 2006. They also claimed that he was the very spy to inspire Ian Fleming's character of James Bond. Despite critics pointing out that Smithers' influence was never confirmed and that there have been numerous claims to the original 007, various coincidences back the *FT*'s claim. The golden typewriter owned by Peter Smithers' wife, the American heiress Dojean Sayman, made an appearance in *Goldfinger*, which also features a villain named Smithers. And there is a laboratory assistant named Smithers in the Bond films *For Your Eyes Only* and *Octopussy*.

While we will never know the answer for sure, at least Smithers' passion for horticulture can easily be explained. Both spying and gardening demand meticulous planning, lots of patience and a knack for digging deep.

Address Water Close Garden, off 34 Colebrook Street, Winchester, SO23 9LH | **Getting there** A 17-minute walk from Winchester railway station | **Hours** Accessible 24 hours | **Tip** A James Bond fan? The National Motor Museum in Beaulieu, 40 mins from Winchester, showcases the Jaguar XKR used in the film *Die Another Day*.

93_Watercress Line

Letting off steam

As the distant toot of a whistle echoes in the countryside, the passengers on the platform fall silent. Some stand up, others simply crane their neck, but all fix their gaze on the point where the train tracks twist and disappear. Moments later, the colossal engine rolls into view, its giant wheels turning in rhythmic symphony. Just as she glides past the pedestrian bridge, the fireman must have shovelled a load of coal into the firebox, for a postcard-perfect puff of white cloud escapes the chimney – making the child in nearly every passenger jump with enthusiasm. 'This,' says Operations Manager Richard Bentley, stepping off the train, 'is 506, one of our oldest engines.' Built in October 1920, she worked through World War II, and is now one of 16 steam engines that pull beautifully restored carriages through rolling hills along a 10-mile track from Alresford to Alton. The Watercress Line, seven miles from Winchester, offers day trips as well as tours for school groups, afternoon tea and murder mysteries, and a light show at Christmas.

Historically, it was much more. 'The Watercress Line,' says Richard Bentley, 'was a game changer.' When the Mid-Hants Railway (its official name) opened in 1865, goods that had previously travelled two or three days by horse and cart or canal boat could now reach the markets of London in a matter of hours. This was vital for the watercress – the leafy green, peppery vegetable that grows so well in and around Alresford. 'Watercress is highly perishable. So quick transport is essential.'

With the rise of road networks, the line fell into decline. In 1973, it was closed and the tracks sold. However, thanks to the passion of volunteers, four years later the first three miles between Alresford and Ropley reopened as a heritage service. 'I see us as custodians,' says Richard. 'Preserving old knowledge and allowing people to step back in time.'

Address The Watercress Line, Railway Station, Alresford, SO24 9JG | **Getting there** Take bus 64 from Winchester, Broadway, to Broad Street, then a short walk | **Hours** Trains run Thu–Sun (term time), Tue–Sun (school holidays); Alresford Station open 9am–4.30pm on service days | **Tip** In Alton, make sure to stop at the Curtis Museum, which offers one of the finest local history collections in Hampshire.

94 Wayfarer's Dole

A taste of kindness at the Hospital of St Cross

Nine hundred years is a long time for things to change. However, at Winchester's Hospital of St Cross, one medieval tradition has outlasted the passage of time. If you ask at the Porter's Lodge for the 'Wayfarer's Dole', Roger Ossa Trivino will reach beneath the counter to retrieve a round wooden plate and a small horn cup. With the aid of tongs, he delicately lifts a piece of malt bread from a stone bread bin onto the plate and pours a large sip of dark ale into the cup.

The Wayfarer's Dole is a charitable act of hospitality that dates back to Henry de Blois, former Bishop of Winchester and grandson of William the Conqueror. One day during the civil war in the early 12th century, Henry de Blois is said to have been walking along the water meadows of the River Itchen when he came across a young farm girl, who begged him for help as her people were starving. Finding the remains of a religious house a little further along the river, he decided to use the site to help the poor. Founded in 1132, the Hospital of St Cross and Almshouse of Noble Poverty is today regarded as the oldest, continually operating almshouse in the country. To this day, 25 brothers are given shelter within the grounds.

The hospital, however, is also open to the public. The chapel (really too grand for such a name) is an example of magnificent 12th-century architecture and if you enter on 14 September, the Feast of the Holy Cross, the sun will fall directly upon the carved cross in one of the vast columns. The Master's Garden offers not only a beautiful array of flowers but also a serene calmness you won't want to leave. At the end of your visit, you might consider asking for the Wayfarer's Dole. Be aware that it is only offered if requested. Standing beneath the stone arch next to the Porter's Lodge, you will find the bread is soft, and the beer wonderfully refreshing – even if you don't normally drink this kind of beverage. This must be the taste of kindness, which is always exquisite.

Address The Hospital of St Cross, St Cross Back Street, SO23 9SD | Getting there Take bus 1 to The Bell Inn, then a 4-minute walk | Hours 1 Apr–31 Oct Mon–Sat 9.30am–5pm, Sun 1–5pm; 1 Nov–31 Mar, Mon–Sat 10.30am–3.30pm | Tip Before you leave, take in the serene atmosphere and scenic views of nearby Saint Cross Park.

95 The Well Worn

Giving fabulous clothes a second chance

As Emma Shaw opens the door to her little studio, you don't know where to look first: the colourful coats and gingham dresses hanging in dense rows on portable hangers, the photos, sketches and notes pinned on the wall, or the big pattern cards on the little workstation. If a scrapbook could be a room, it would be the atelier of The Well Worn.

The idea came to Emma Shaw quite unexpectedly after 20 years of intense work in the British fashion industry. Having started in a knitwear factory in Manchester, she had worked her way up to the position of design director at FatFace by the late 2010s, when she decided to take a sabbatical to spend more time with her son. During that break, she found a slower pace and realised she wanted the clothes she created to be slower as well. What if, she thought, something well worn, could be *worn well* again? A pre-loved pair of jeans, a sweater, a blouse – not to be hidden at the back of a wardrobe, but worn on a day out with giddying joy?

In May 2022, Emma took the plunge. In the beginning, she designed little scarves out of indigo fabric. Soon, denim jeans and jackets followed, patched up and adorned with cute stitches. Before long, her first dress followed, Florentine, which was technically not made out of pre-used fabric but of Ecovera, a sustainable viscose cloth.

Five years later, Emma Shaw's work is so popular, she is working with seamstresses in other parts of Hampshire and her upcycled items are ordered from countries as far afield as Japan and Australia. At a time when British fashion production had moved abroad, she brought her atelier back to the city of Winchester. 'Something that was last done by Burberry,' she says. In her first-floor studio in Middle Brook Street, she not only creates clothes herself but shares her knowledge in little workshops with others. Making the fashion world better, one little stitch at a time.

Address The Well Worn, 1st Floor Studio, 4b Middle Brook Street, SO23 8AQ, www.thewellworn.co.uk | Getting there A 5-minute walk from Winchester bus station | Hours Open by appointment, see website for details | Tip Before or after your appointment, stop at the Open House Deli downstairs for a delicious cappuccino.

96 West Hill Cemetery

Murder on the British Express

Flickering gaslight illuminated Hackney Station on the evening of 9 July 1864, when at 10.11pm a train pulled in and two bank clerks entered the first-class carriage. As they sat down, they noticed blood stains on the upholstery. Alarmed, they alerted the guard, who discovered more blood, as well as a black beaver hat, a bag and a walking stick. Meanwhile, the driver of a passing train applied the brakes. Stepping onto the tracks, he found the senior bank clerk Thomas Briggs critically wounded. The 69-year-old would not survive the night.

In that moment, 39 years after the invention of the passenger steam locomotive, the first murder on a British railway had taken place. Unsurprisingly, the media erupted in a frenzy, the public was terrified, and Scotland Yard called upon one of their best: 34-year-old Inspector Richard Tanner.

The motive was quickly established: Briggs' gold watch, his chain and gold eyeglasses were missing – robbery! A jeweller then gave a description of a German who had exchanged a gold chain. A cabman identified the hat; he had bought it for a Franz Müller, who had once been engaged to his daughter and was now en route to New York.

Tanner did not hesitate. He boarded a faster steamship, despite the ongoing American Civil War making New York an unwelcoming place for a British investigator. Yet, Tanner persisted. Upon Müller's arrival, he was arrested. In his possession were Briggs' watch and hat. Back in England, Müller was publicly executed, and, in the aftermath, all train carriages were fitted with communication cords, allowing passengers to contact the driver.

You can find Richard Tanner's grave within West Hill Cemetery. Enter at St James Lane, keep to the right and walk uphill for a few metres. You will find the grave to your left – and accompanying it, a sweeping view over the Itchen Valley.

Address West Hill Cemetery, Winchester, SO22 4NX | Getting there A 14-minute walk from Winchester railway station | Hours Daily 7am–10pm | Tip Want a behind-the-scenes look at the police and fire services? The Hampshire Police and Fire Heritage Trust runs a little museum on the second floor of the Solent Sky Museum in Southampton.

97_Westgate Museum

Look up!

While historical work often leads us to dig deep, to surmise what is below us, one of Winchester's most atmospheric museums can be found high up: the Westgate Museum is – as its name suggests – situated in one of the two surviving medieval gates of Winchester. From a semi-circular wooden door, steep stone steps lead through a curved passage past walls oozing with the cool and calm composure often found in centuries-old constructions. The museum might only consist of one room, but the atmosphere that dances between ancient oak beams and thick walls is so dense that one room provides a lasting impression.

To discover a particularly stunning souvenir, look up! The intricately painted oak ceiling squares show profiles of possibly Tudor and Roman noblemen as well as the monogram 'I W'. The letters stand for John White, the warden of Winchester College from 1542 to 1554. It is understood that he commissioned this frieze to celebrate the marriage of Mary Tudor and Philip of Spain, which took place at Winchester Cathedral on 25 July 1554; an important day for a city that had seen a decline in royal events in the decades before, and a nod to its rich history. The wedding was a lavish affair – the Cathedral, for instance, was 'richly hanged with arras and cloth of gold' – not only because it celebrated the marriage of England's first regnant queen but also to send a signal of strength to the Spanish, curbing any ideas of invasion. But although the newlywed couple visited the college, it is unlikely they ever saw the painted panels.

Before you leave, head up one more time. Follow a further, very narrow set of steps upstairs and you reach the roof of the gate. The little platform at the north end allows you one of the most stunning views over Winchester High Street, framed by the lush crowns of St Giles Hill.

Address Westgate Museum, High Street, Winchester, SO23 9AP | Getting there A 7-minute walk from Winchester railway station | Hours Daily 10am–5pm | Tip Stop for a hot drink and snack at The Round Table Café and Gift Shop, new at The Great Hall.

98_Whitchurch Silk Mill

Weaving history at the UK's oldest working mill

In the quaint town of Whitchurch on the River Test sits a proud Georgian mill. Built in 1815, it was opened in 1817 as a silk mill due to the economic downturn that hit England after the Napoleonic Wars, when silk weaving offered a lifeline to the mill. Today it is the oldest continuously operating silk mill in England. Stepping over a clear chalk stream, you pass the working waterwheel to enter the historic building and start your tour on the second floor.

The looms can weave about five metres of silk a day but preparing them is a meticulous process. First, silk threads, dyed in vibrant colours, are wound onto bobbins on the top floor. These are arranged on a warping mill to form a warp of parallel threads, which are rolled onto a large wooden beam. The beam is then fitted onto one of the historic looms on the ground floor. Many of them were installed in the early 19th century by James Hide, who was Thomas Burberry's nephew. For decades, these looms produced silk in 22 different colours for the iconic linings of Burberry's trench-coats. These days, the weavers create ribbons for the Jane Austen House and silk for the George Washington suit to commemorate the Declaration of Independence in 2026.

Would you give it a try? Taking a seat at the visitor loom, you need to place a foot on one treadle. Instantly, a row of silk threads lifts, leaving a gap for the shuttle to pass through. As you do so, the weft thread is pulled along. Once the shuttle reaches the other side, you must beat the weft thread to align with the already woven piece of fabric. A complex yet satisfying task.

Nearby, weavers are deep in conversation with their trainee. Although their talk is light hearted, it is a matter of national significance: they are two of the last five silk ribbon weavers in Britain.

Address Whitchurch Silk Mill, 28 Winchester Street, RG28 7AL, www.whitchurchsilkmill.org.uk | Getting there Take bus 75 to Andover, then bus 76 to The Square, Whitchurch, then a short walk | Hours Tue–Sun & Bank Holidays 10.30am–5pm | Tip After your visit, pop into the antique shops in the Little Chapel a couple of doors down and perhaps find one of the lovely watercolours by Jo South.

99 The William Walker

How a diver saved Winchester Cathedral

The city of Winchester is neither a port city, nor situated next to a lake. Yet one of its most central pubs displays a diver's head to commemorate a man who helped to save the city's most famous landmark. In 1905, deep-sea diver William Walker was called into the city from the Royal Navy Dockyard in Portsmouth to prevent Winchester Cathedral from sinking.

Winchester Cathedral is built on very soft ground. It stands on the floodplain of the River Itchen so the soil is prone to a high underlying water table (which still regularly floods the crypt). Because of that, in the early 1900s, deep cracks began to appear in the church walls. It is said that some of them were big enough for owls to roost in, and lumps of rocks would crash onto the floor.

In a first attempt to stabilise the building, architect Thomas Jackson wanted to underpin it with a modern foundation. But the workers could not fill the trenches they dug with concrete as instructed because they were flooded with water almost immediately. Finally, engineer Francis Fox had the brilliant idea: if the water could not be kept away, why not bring someone in who was used to working with it?

From 1906 to 1911, William Walker descended into the waters underneath the cathedral. He worked six hours a day, in absolute darkness, in trenches that were up to six metres deep; wearing a heavy diving suit that took so long to get out of that at lunchtime he usually just took off his helmet. Working without gloves, he was forces to navigate the muddy, cloudy water with his bare hands. In the six years, he put more than 25,000 bags of cement into place. These would, together with the newly erected buttresses, finally give the cathedral its necessary stability. In 1912, the cathedral honoured his work with a thanksgiving service, and to this day the city keeps his memory alive with a cosy pub that bears his name.

Address The William Walker, 34 The Square, Winchester, SO23 9EX | Getting there A 13-minute walk from Winchester railway station | Hours Mon & Tue 11am–10pm, Wed & Thu 11am–11pm, Fri & Sat 11am–11.30pm, Sun noon–10pm | Tip For more information about William Walker, there is a brilliant, family-friendly Diving Museum in Gosport, just 45 minutes from Winchester.

100 Winchester Bible

Finest layers of medieval art

Winchester Cathedral's arguably most prized treasure lies behind a striking and ornate wooden door at the southeastern side of the church. Stepping into the Kings & Scribes exhibition in the South Transept, you see vast volumes in spacious display boxes. Even from a slight distance, the thick, slightly rippled pages seem to murmur with voices of past centuries.

Around 1160, the Benedictine monks of Old Minster – probably commissioned by Henry de Blois, the grandson of William the Conqueror – began their work on a new Bible, one that should be written in Vulgate Latin (a 4th-century translation that was preferred across Europe at that time) and that should be decorated so lavishly it would exceed all its precursors.

Eight hundred and fifty years later, the Winchester Bible still surpasses its competitors and has even been called 'a candidate for the greatest work of art produced in England' by art historian Christopher de Hamel. Over a period of at least four years, one individual monk carefully copied the text in neat columns onto both sides of 468 calfskin folios, each of them more than 1.5 feet long. Once the text was completed, a team of six highly skilled artists created vibrant illuminations, using powdered gold, vermilion and lapis lazuli that still shimmer today. Initially, around 100 illustrations were planned, but only around half of them were realised.

Bizarrely, only one of the two full-page illustrations remains in Winchester. The other was probably removed around 1820, and was allegedly offered to the celebrated designer William Morris for £100 by an Italian collector. As Morris could not afford it, it was sold instead to financier John Pierpont Morgan. Ironically, the page would have ended up in this library if Morris had purchased it, since the financier later also bought the designer's own collection. It can today be found in The Morgan Library & Museum in New York.

Address Kings & Scribes Exhibition, Winchester Cathedral, 9 The Close, SO23 9LS, www.winchester-cathedral.org.uk | **Getting there** A 7-minute walk from Winchester bus station | **Hours** Mon–Sat 10.30am–4.30pm, Sun 12.30–2.30pm | **Tip** The second most fascinating aspect of the Kings & Scribes Exhibition is the Morley Library, which offers more than 3,000 books and 40 manuscripts, some from as early as the medieval period.

101 Winchester Cathedral

The world's longest medieval church

Although now standing slightly to the east of Winchester, no other building takes centre stage in this city like its cathedral does. Started in 1079 by Bishop Walkelin and consecrated on 15 July, St Swithun's Day, in 1093, it is the longest intact medieval church in the world, and the longest Gothic cathedral in Europe. As the seat of the bishops of Winchester, whose vast estates in medieval times endowed them with more political power than any other churchmen in England, the cathedral gave rise to other powerful institutions in its vicinity. Its interior is known to millions around the world, even to those who have never set foot inside it, as the cathedral stood in for St Paul's Cathedral as well as Westminster Abbey in *The Crown*. It also appeared in films such as *The Da Vinci Code* and *Elizabeth: The Golden Age* as well as the TV miniseries *Wolf Hall*.

As befits a grand cathedral, it houses numerous prized possessions: the fragments of St Swithun's shrine, the oldest, substantially unaltered medieval quire (a beautiful example with intricate wood carvings), the chair believed to have been used by Mary Tudor during her wedding to Philip of Spain, and Jane Austen's grave, which can be found in the north aisle. Yet its most surreal memorial is something we can no longer properly see.

The giant West Window does not depict biblical scenes but rather a haphazard mosaic, which dates back to the English Civil War. In December 1642, Roundhead soldiers charged into the cathedral on horseback. Hoping for earthly treasures, they ransacked the relics, but found little except bones. Furiously, they began throwing them through the windows. Once the soldiers had left, the good people of Winchester rushed to the scene, picking up the shards of glass. They hid them in their homes until the monarchy was restored 18 years later, and the church window could be rebuilt from the recovered fragments.

Address Winchester Cathedral, 9 The Close, SO23 9LS, www.winchester-cathedral.org.uk | Getting there A 7-minute walk from Winchester bus station | Hours Mon–Sat 9am–5pm, Sun 12.30–3pm | Tip Fascinated by church buildings? Visit Winchester offers a self-guided Itchen-Valley-Churches-Trail (see www.visitwinchester.co.uk).

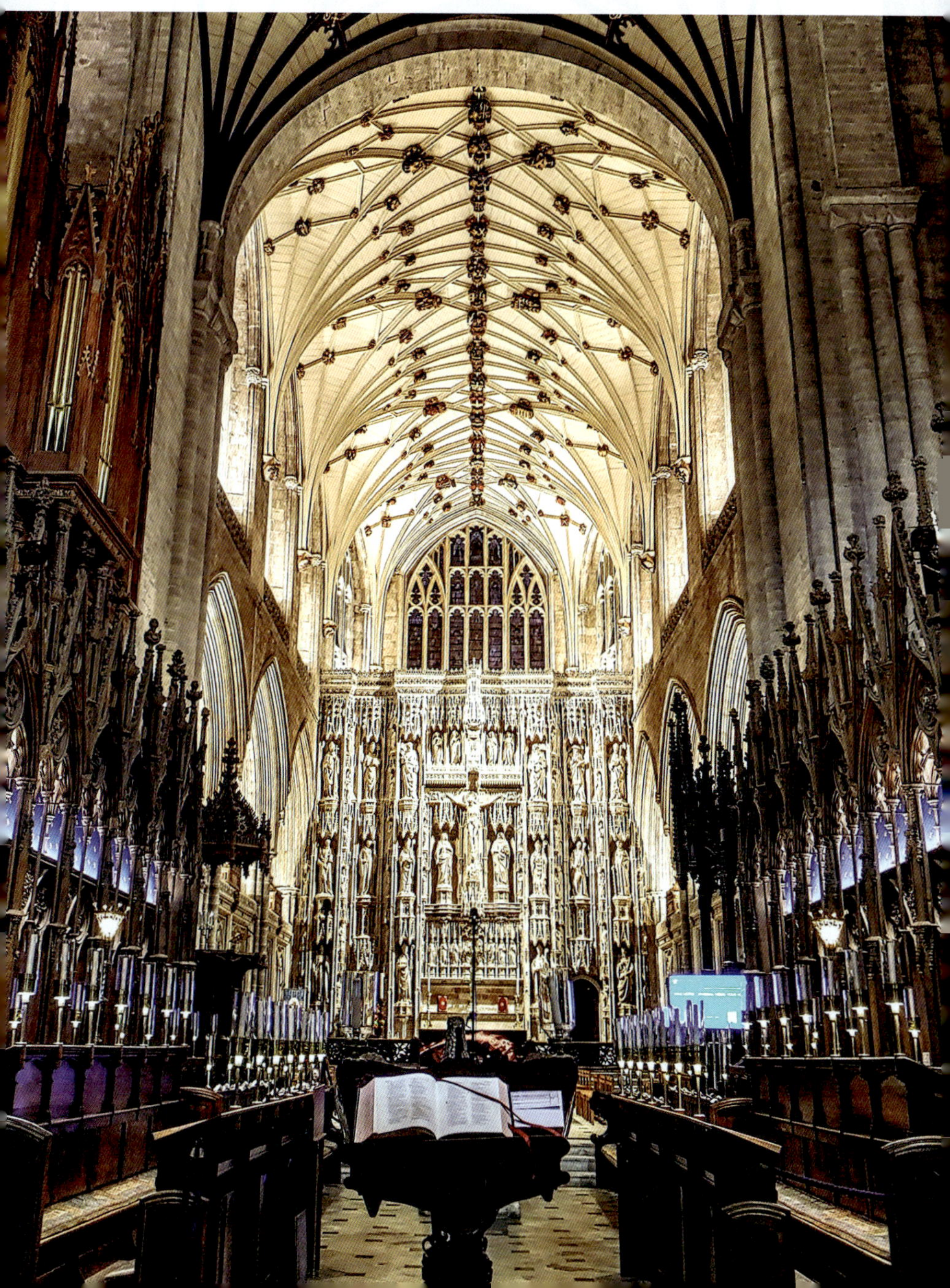

102 Winchester Christmas Market

England's (perhaps) most magical winter fair

The Christmas season simply isn't the Christmas season if you haven't hung a wreath on your front door, watched *Love Actually* at least once and enjoyed a cup of mulled wine amid the dazzling surroundings of a Christmas market. With its alpine wooden chalets, beautiful copper urns and the cathedral shining atmospherically beside it, is there a more magical place to do that in England than Winchester Christmas Market? It was voted Best Christmas Market of the UK in 2020 and regularly ranks among the top festive markets of Europe.

One of the first people to be approached when the idea took shape in 2006 was Marcelo Pugliese. Only the previous year, he had taken over The Old Vine in Great Minster Street, transforming the slightly run-down pub into a thriving pub-restaurant and lovingly restoring its century-old rooms for overnight guests. Could he imagine offering mulled wine in one of the chalets? Marcelo didn't need to be asked twice.

Reviving an old family recipe from his German ancestors in Düsseldorf, he and his team set up in chalet number 13, serving steaming cups of spiced wine. (The vital secret ingredients, if you can keep them to yourself, are juniper berries to balance the sweetness and ginger to add a touch of sharpness.) The offering – not just of mulled wine but of the atmospheric market with its lights, festively presented local crafts and produce as well as enchanting Christmas concerts – was so well received that it quickly became Winchester's most iconic festival. And The Old Vine's mulled wine chalet turned into a seasonal staple. Today, The Old Vine offers not only spiced wine but also mulled cider and hot chocolate, complete with whipped cream and marshmallows, which somehow tastes even more wonderful in front of the illuminated cathedral than when watching *Love Actually* at home.

Address Winchester Christmas Market, 9 The Close, SO23 9LS | **Getting there** A 7-minute walk from Winchester bus station | **Hours** End Nov–22 Dec, Mon–Wed 10am–6pm, Thu 10am–7pm, Fri & Sat 10am–8pm, Sun 10am–5pm | **Tip** If you want to enjoy mulled wine on Christmas Eve (when the market is already closed), drop in to The Old Vine itself.

103 Winchester City Museum

A medieval tale of water, waste and justice

Winchester City Museum is not short of prized artefacts. It displays jewellery from the Roman Empire, a magnificent model of the city during Victorian times and two purses that once belonged to Jane Austen. Thus, it may surprise you that an item tied to a major medieval lawsuit still shaping modern human rights was found in a latrine pit. The toilet seat of John de Tytynge, to be found in the domestic life section, stands as a reminder of a row between a rich merchant and a persistent washerwoman, the outcome of which resulted in an international legal obligation we are still benefitting from today. It was also a lesson that we should never shy away from righting a wrong.

In 1299, John de Tytynge, then one of the richest merchants in the city, resided in Schuldwortstrete, today known as Upper Brook Street. A little bit downstream in the same street lived Juliana de la Floude. Working in a launderette, it came as a shock to her when John de Tytynge dammed the brook for his own purposes. Without clean, fresh water, Juliana could not carry out her profession, and would lose her vital income. She was furious. After all, water was a common good. And thus, she complained – to the king.

Oh, but what was she thinking? That a monarch would side with a simple washerwoman? That the king would reprimand one of the richest merchants of the city? That the twice-elected mayor had to comply with the commands of a common resident? Indeed, this is precisely what happened. In a writ dated 5 August 1299, King Edward I commanded the mayors and bailiffs of Winchester to 'make those men cease their unwarranted obstruction' and to ensure 'that Juliana has the kind of convenient access to that watercourse that she ought and that she and her predecessors were accustomed to have in times past'. This ruling later became part of the UN Convention of Human Rights, providing the legal basis for freshwater access to billions of people.

Address Winchester City Museum, The Square, Winchester, SO23 9ES | Getting there A 12-minute walk from Winchester railway station | Hours Jan–Mar Mon–Fri 10am–4pm, Sat 10am–5pm, Sun 11am–5pm; Apr–Dec Mon–Sat 10am–5pm, Sun 11am–5pm | Tip The Winchester Tourist Guides offer a superb tour exploring the Hidden Waterways of Winchester (www.winchestertouristguides.com).

104 Winchester Coffee Roasters

How to make the perfect brew

'See the mouse tail?' Jemma Maguire asks. The group leans in for a better view as the espresso flows in a thin, steady stream from the spout of the basket into a shot glass. 'This is what we aim for.' As the light-coloured froth on top reaches the measure line, Jemma pulls the lever. 'You should stop just as the espresso starts to pale, usually after 24 to 28 seconds.' The group nods, focused. Then, it is their turn.

Making a cup of coffee is an everyday task in most British households. But making good quality espresso is an art form. An art form, nevertheless, that Mark Goulding is intent on making accessible to the public. In 2012, after having trained and worked with some of the best baristas in Australia, he started to roast his own coffee in his garage, selling the beans at Winchester Farmers' Market. But sure enough, beans are only one factor: different types of machines and brewing techniques need a different coarseness, and certain beans work better for espressos, others for cappuccinos.

Today, the Winchester Coffee Roasters train not only those who are keen to work in cafés or restaurants, but also those who want to create the perfect brew at home. In two hours, the participants find out which regions create which coffee flavours (if you favour chocolatey notes, beans from Asia might be what you are looking for); the correct amount of ground beans in the portafilter basket (18 grams); or the ideal temperature of milk when being frothed (65 degrees). By the end of the two hours, the foam you frothed glides smoothly into the cup, blending with the dark espresso brewed earlier and even leaving a delicate leaf pattern on top. Your pride is only slightly dampened, when pro barista Pat Malec hands you a cappuccino – featuring a seahorse design. At least he concedes, 'I have been practising this design for years.'

Address Winchester Coffee Roasters, 7a Sun Valley Business Park, Winnall, Winchester, SO23 0LB | Getting there A 28-minute walk from Winchester station or take bus 2 to Winnall Manor Road | Hours Advance booking essential (www.winchestercoffeeschool.co.uk) | Tip Not time to make it out to Winnall? The South Downs Social in Middle Brook Street uses the Coffee Roasters beans.

105_Winchester College

Manners maketh man

When thinking of the most prestigious boarding school in the country, a short four-letter word may come to mind. But while Eton College rose to considerable fame due to royal and prime ministerial connections, the title of oldest, continuously running school in England goes to Winchester College. Indeed, Henry VI didn't just use Winchester as his model when founding his school near Windsor in 1440, he even took soil from Hampshire to build Eton – metaphorically as well as literally on Winchester's foundations.

Winchester College was founded in 1382 by William of Wykeham – a name locals come across frequently, perhaps without knowing quite how extraordinary he was. Wykeham, Bishop of Winchester as well as Chancellor of England, had come from a poor background. It was probably the support of wealthy patrons that allowed him to have an academic education. He entered King Edward's service, and rose to be his most trusted assistant, but he never forgot his roots.

In his fifties, Wykeham had a radical idea: a school not just for the wealthy but for bright yet poor boys who had little chance of continuing their education. Up to 70 scholars should receive their educational foundations in Winchester before moving on to New College Oxford (which Wykeham had also created). His opinion that people should not be judged by their birth or status but by their actions is still embedded in the college's crest. It is neither in French (which was spoken by the court), nor in Latin (which was the language of the clergy) but in plain English: *Manners maketh man.*

Little nods to his motto can be found all over the school. Tour guide Kate Mills points to the bottom of the grand church windows in the college's chapel. 'Do you see these little figures? These are neither bishops, nor kings, but secular workers.' A fitting reflection of Wykeham's belief that character, not status, makes the man.

Address Winchester College, College Street, Winchester, SO23 9NA | **Getting there** A 12-minute walk from Winchester bus station | **Hours** Free, 60-minute tours daily 2.15pm & 3.30pm; in-depth tours on specific topics also available (see www.winchestercollege.org/visit-us/guided-tours for details) | **Tip** Take a walk along the college grounds past the River Itchen and stop at The Queen Inn on your way back.

106 Winchester College Treasury

The Sorting Cup

Cups are often bestowed with particular prestige: think of the Cup of Christ, the holy chalice used by Jesus during the Last Supper, considered one of the most sacred relics in Christian tradition; the World Cup, which is in various sports regarded as the apex of achievement; in Persian mythology, the Cup of Jamshid, associated with divination; and in English culture, the cup of tea – a representation of social rituals. However, there is one vessel that should not be missed in this list: Winchester College's Election Cup.

Election at Winchester College is a unique process. Through a series of written exams as well as interviews, the Warden and Fellows of the college elect so-called scholars. Historically these 70 boys received a free education; today they are among the brightest pupils of each year. The scholars are lodged in the oldest boarding house, and are easily distinguished from the 'commoners' (those students who historically paid for their commons, the provision of meals and accommodation) through the gowns they wear whenever they are on campus (but never in town).

In 1555, former warden John White presented the college with a magnificent silver cup, which he wished to be used during the election process in the future. Today, this vessel is one of the best-preserved medieval cups in the country. You can find it in one of the display cases of the college's treasury, for in 2016 the medieval stables of the school were turned into a museum. Here, you can study Chinese ceramics from the Han to the Qing dynasty, stunning Ancient Greek vases, casts of the Parthenon frieze, and parts of the college's silver collection. But be aware that for two days in May and September, you will look for the cup in vain: while no longer in use as a vessel to drink from, the cup is still present during the election process.

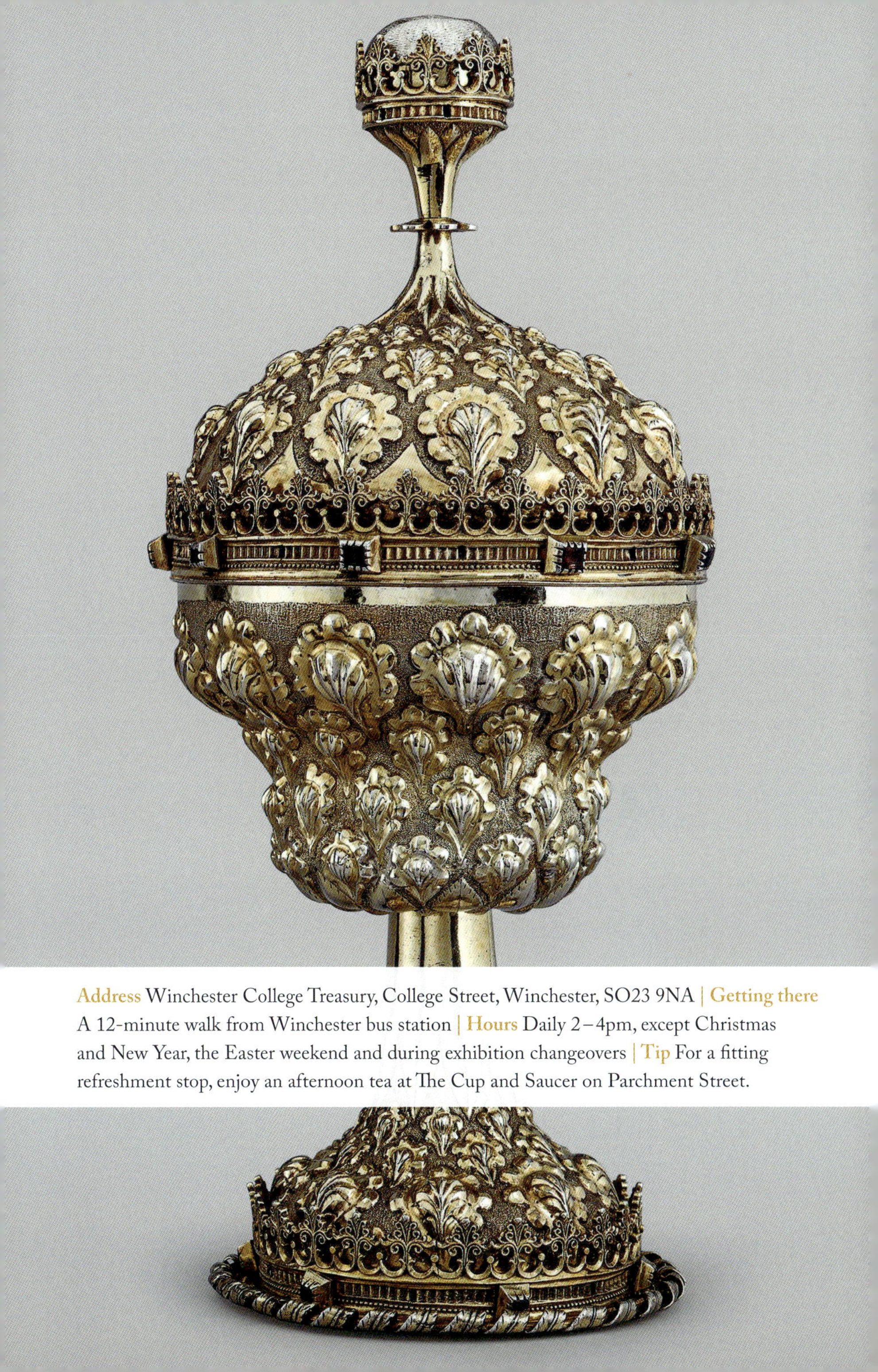

Address Winchester College Treasury, College Street, Winchester, SO23 9NA | Getting there A 12-minute walk from Winchester bus station | Hours Daily 2–4pm, except Christmas and New Year, the Easter weekend and during exhibition changeovers | Tip For a fitting refreshment stop, enjoy an afternoon tea at The Cup and Saucer on Parchment Street.

107 Winchester Prison

The tragedy of sweet Fanny Adams

The public hanging of Frederick Baker on 24 December 1867 is remembered not only because it was the last public hanging in front of Winchester Prison, but also because it followed one of the most brutal crimes ever committed in Hampshire.

On 24 August, eight-year-old Fanny Adams from Tanhouse Lane in Alton went out with her younger sister Lizzie and their friend Minnie Warner. As the three children walked towards the Flood Meadow, they were approached by a man in a black coat. He offered Minnie three halfpence if she would take young Lizzie to play, and promised Fanny a halfpenny if she would come with him, up The Hollow. Fanny Adams took the money but refused to accompany him. At that point, the man picked her up against her will and carried her into a nearby hopfield.

When Minnie and Lizzie returned home without Fanny a few hours later, Mrs Adams rushed towards The Hollow and did, indeed, encounter the man in a coat. He introduced himself in a respectable manner as the clerk of a local solicitor, confirmed that he had given the children money but assured her that Fanny had returned safely. But when Fanny failed to come home, a search party was started. The eight-year-old was found murdered and horrifically mutilated in the hopfield.

When Superintendent William Cheyney arrested the solicitor's clerk, Frederick Baker, at his office, the man feigned innocence. He offered implausible justifications for his wet shoes, the bloodstains on his shirt, the little knife in his pocket and even his diary entry, which read: '24th August, Saturday – killed a young girl. It was fine and hot.'

But then a local painter found a large stone in the hopfield with marks of blood, long hair and bits of flesh – possibly the murder weapon. At his trial, the jury found him guilty within 15 minutes. Frederick Baker was hanged on Christmas Eve in front of 5,000 people.

Address HMP Winchester, Romsey Road, Winchester, SO22 5DF | Getting there An 18-minute walk from Winchester railway station | Hours Viewable from the outside only – unless you are serving a sentence | Tip Have a stroll through the hidden St James Cemetery across the road from the prison.

108 Winchester Science Centre

Explore UK's largest standalone planetarium

It is the moment astronomer Anna Gammon-Ross loves the most: when she hits the button on her control panel and the large auditorium dips into darkness before the first 'Oooh!' echoes through the rows as the stars appear on the giant domed ceiling. 'It is magical, isn't it?' she whispers. It is, indeed, a wonderfully immersive experience – but then, we are in the country's biggest standalone planetarium. Opened in 2008 as part of the Winchester Science Centre, the 176-seat auditorium is topped with an 18-yard-diameter dome, which takes audiences on interactive journeys through space. Although the shows are geared towards children between three and twelve, they never fail to impress attending adults, too.

Taking a laser pointer, Anna highlights four stars positioned in a cross. 'This is Cygnus.' As she speaks, two lines appear, connecting the four stars into that very cross. 'It is also called the Swan Constellation.' At the press of another button, an illustration appears: layered over the cross, a swan spreads its wings. 'This is one of the brightest constellations. So, it is easy to see even in a place with more light pollution.' Smoothly, the astronomer guides you through constellations before shooting past millions of stars in a matter of seconds. Suddenly, the familiar rings of Saturn fill the bottom half of the dome. 'Did you know, this planet has 274 moons?'

Growing up in Norfolk, Anna was always fascinated by the night sky. These days, she helps inquisitive children satisfy their curiosity. 'Children love the gory details.' One question that comes up often: what happens if you fall into a black hole. And, indeed, what would happen? 'Around a black hole, gravity is so strong that whatever part of you heads towards it first would get massively pulled. This process,' Anna grins, 'has a brilliant scientific name: spaghettification.'

Address Winchester Science Centre, Telegraph Way, SO21 1HZ, www.winchestersciencecentre.org | **Getting there** Take bus 64 to Science Centre | **Hours** Daily 9.30am–5pm weekends and school holidays | **Tip** In Stoney Lane, a blue plaque remembers the famous local astronomer Alfred Curtis, who built an observatory in his own garden.

109__Winnall Moors

Need for reed

Can you hear it, this soft *churr-churr-churr-chip* that seems to come directly from the reeds? It is the sound of the reed warbler, a little bird with a warm brown coat and pale throat that likes to weave its nest as a sling between reed stems. Ah, and listen to this energetic 'scratchy' song, as if someone were recounting a story! It comes from the sedge warbler, whose darker coat appears busier and whose males never repeat a song in their effort to impress the females.

With its 64 hectares of natural floodplain, Winnall Moors Wildlife Trust Nature Reserve – less than a 15-minute walk from Winchester City Centre – is the ideal place if you want to reconnect with nature. It is a peaceful place: no dogs, no bikes, no swimming, just you and the wild. Entering through a solid oak gate, you are led along a gravel path next to the River Itchen before a boardwalk carries you deep into the reeds. Once, this area was part of Hyde Abbey and featured St Gertrude's Chapel. In the 1800s and 1900s, a network of ditches was dug to allow water to flood the meadows, creating lush grass for the grazing sheep. As these meadows were never altered with artificial fertiliser, they were able to develop into vibrant grassland – rich in flowers and wildlife.

Today, it is a feast for the senses – even in the serenity of winter when the earth is crisp and you might catch a deer dashing in and out of the woods. But particularly on warm summer days, when there are not just the enticing birdsong and the soothing swoosh of the wind playing with the reeds but also the smell of warm soil and clear water, the rough bark of the trees as you trace your fingers along it, and a kaleidoscope of soothing green.

If you are very lucky, you might catch a blue flash just above the river. With its clear water, its quiet perches and its rich wildlife, Winnall Moors is not just ideal for humans, but also for kingfishers.

Address Winnall Moors Wildlife Trust Nature Reserve, Durngate Place, Winchester, SO23 8DX | Getting there A 13-minute walk from Winchester bus station | Hours Usually accessible 24 hours, but sometimes closed for the moving of cattle or during flooding | Tip After your walk, The Willow Tree, with its lush green garden space, offers the ideal venue for refreshments.

110 Wolvesey Castle

The pomp and pipes of bishops

Being one of the most influential and wealthy figures in the country – and as the owner of estates stretching from London to Somerset, one most likely was – requires a residence that combines the fortification of a castle with the grandeur of a palace. Such a home needs not only to be defensible against enemies but also to proclaim one's status. Thus, in 1110 Bishop William Giffard laid the foundation stone of what would become one of the grandest medieval buildings in the country: Wolvesey Palace. Although only ruins remain today, the massive wall of the East Hall still stands as a reminder of its former splendour.

While William Giffard started this process, it would be his successor to whom the credit for this palace was really due. Henry of Blois – former Bishop of Winchester as well as Abbot of Glastonbury (a position he retained even after becoming bishop, because why not have it all?) – was not only a powerful man who could rival the king in power and prestige, he was, in fact, of royal descent: his grandfather was William the Conqueror, and his brother Stephen ruled the country for nearly two decades. So keen was Henry of Blois to maintain the strong presence of the castle that he continued adding to it from the moment he took over as bishop in 1129 until his death 42 years later.

Yet, Wolvesey Castle was not only a symbol of luxury and power, but also a marvel of innovation. Henry oversaw the installation of one of the earliest known examples of piped freshwater supplies. Whilst other castles still relied on a labour-intensive water supply, Henry built a well-house in the centre of the courtyard, from which a pipe ran to an ornamental cistern, with additional pipes distributing water to the southern courtyard and another well-house. The system was so advanced that chronicler Gerald the Welshman noted that Henry had built a 'complex aqueduct'.

Address Wolvesey Castle (Old Bishop's Palace), College Street, Winchester, SO23 9NB | Getting there A 12-minute walk from Winchester bus station | Hours Daily 1 Apr–30 Sep 10am–5pm, 1 Oct–31 Mar 10am–4pm, free entry | Tip Follow the nearby Weir Walk to the charming Weir Gate and watch the water make its way to the Bishop's House.

111 The Wykeham Arms

Collecting moments and memorabilia

As a pub manager, you would want your property to be light and friendly, the windows to offer a clear view of the outside and the streets leading up to the entrance to be clean and clear. Yet one of the most exciting days for Jon Howard as manager of The Wykeham Arms was when the windows were blackened, rubble lay in piles across the street and large wooden beams, obstructing any passing vehicles, were set against the façade.

On 24 January 2016, Netflix re-created a scene set during World War II for the first season of its hit series *The Crown*. What none of the viewers would suspect, when looking at the destroyed red brick road on TV, was that behind the black windows, the cosy pub with its wood panelling and rustic furniture that has served customers since 1755 – and once allegedly even Lord Nelson – was operating as usual. 'Initially, Netflix approached us and asked whether we could close the pub,' Jon Howard remembers. But as it was a Sunday – one of the busiest days for a pub – he managed to arrange a deal, operating the premises behind the scenes. In the end, he was happy he did: after shooting that day's scenes, American actor John Lithgow had his dinner in this very pub. He ordered, of course, a Sunday roast.

It seems fitting that the actor who portrayed Winston Churchill enjoyed his dinner here: among the eclectic mix of hundreds of time-worn tankards, dozens of curious walking sticks and numerous faded paintings, you can find not only paintings and figures of the former prime minister but also an armband and a sceptre worn and carried by the pallbearers at Churchill's state funeral.

The dense collection of nostalgia was started by the previous landlord Graham Jameson. Jon Howard points to a picture of him on the wall, where famous former patrons are remembered. The picture of Graham shows him in his iconic demeanour: with a bowtie and a glass of red wine in hand.

Address The Wykeham Arms, 75 Kingsgate Street, Winchester, SO23 9PE | Getting there A 10-minute walk from Winchester bus station | Hours Mon–Sat 11am–11pm, Sun 11am–10pm | Tip Fancy a glass of wine for later? There is a gorgeous wine shop and delicatessen – Kingsgate Wine & Provisions – just opposite the pub.

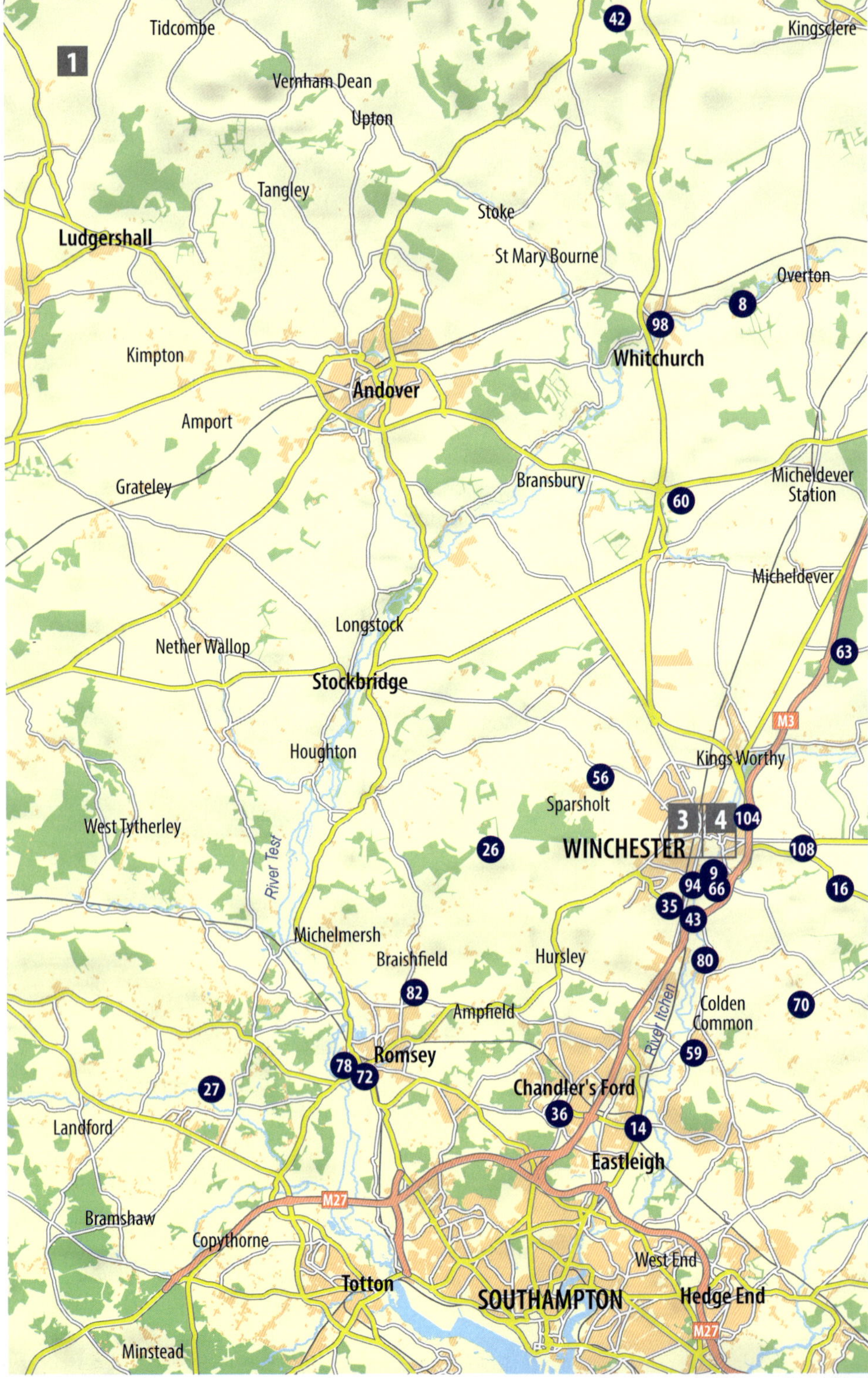
1
Tidcombe
Kingsclere
Vernham Dean
Upton
Tangley
Stoke
Ludgershall
St Mary Bourne
Overton
Whitchurch
Kimpton
Andover
Amport
Grateley
Bransbury
Micheldever Station
Micheldever
Longstock
Nether Wallop
Stockbridge
M3
Kings Worthy
Houghton
Sparsholt
West Tytherley
WINCHESTER
River Test
Michelmersh
Braishfield
Hursley
Ampfield
River Itchen
Colden Common
Romsey
Chandler's Ford
Landford
Eastleigh
M27
Bramshaw
Copythorne
West End
Totton
SOUTHAMPTON
Hedge End
Minstead
3
4
42
98
8
60
63
56
104
108
26
9
94
66
16
35
43
80
82
70
59
78
72
27
36
14

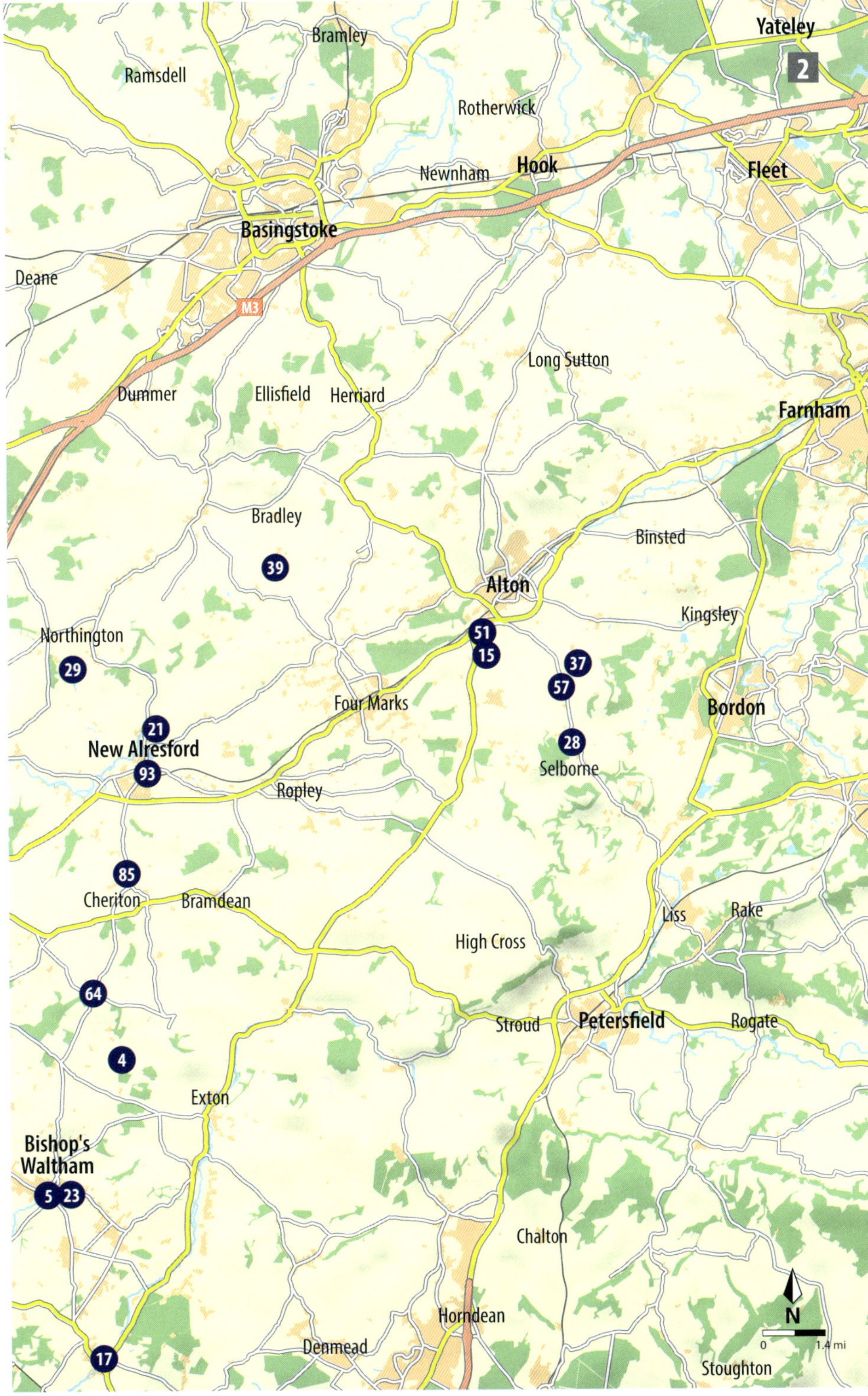
Bramley
Yateley
2
Ramsdell
Rotherwick
Hook
Fleet
Newnham
Basingstoke
Deane
M3
Long Sutton
Dummer
Ellisfield
Herriard
Farnham
Bradley
Binsted
39
Alton
Kingsley
Northington
51
15
37
29
57
Four Marks
Bordon
21
28
New Alresford
Selborne
93
Ropley
85
Cheriton
Bramdean
Liss
Rake
High Cross
64
Stroud
Petersfield
Rogate
4
Exton
Bishop's Waltham
5
23
Chalton
N
Horndean
0
1.4 mi
Denmead
17
Stoughton

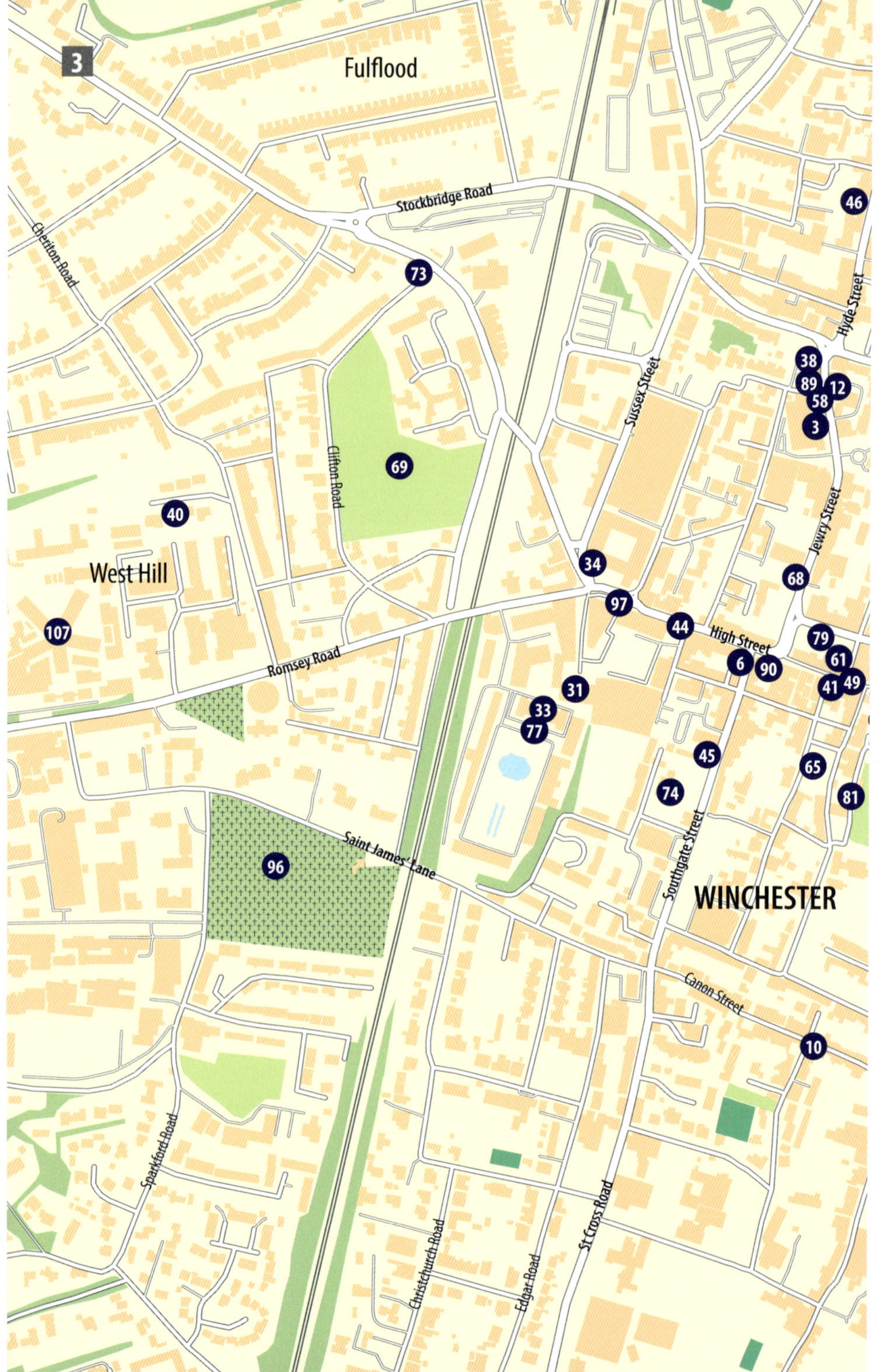
3
Fulflood
Stockbridge Road
Cheriton Road
Hyde Street
Sussex Street
Clifton Road
Jewry Street
West Hill
High Street
Romsey Road
Saint James' Lane
Southgate Street
WINCHESTER
Canon Street
Sparkford Road
St Cross Road
Christchurch Road
Edgar Road
46
73
38
89
12
58
3
69
40
34
68
97
44
107
79
6
90
61
41
49
31
33
77
45
65
74
81
96
10

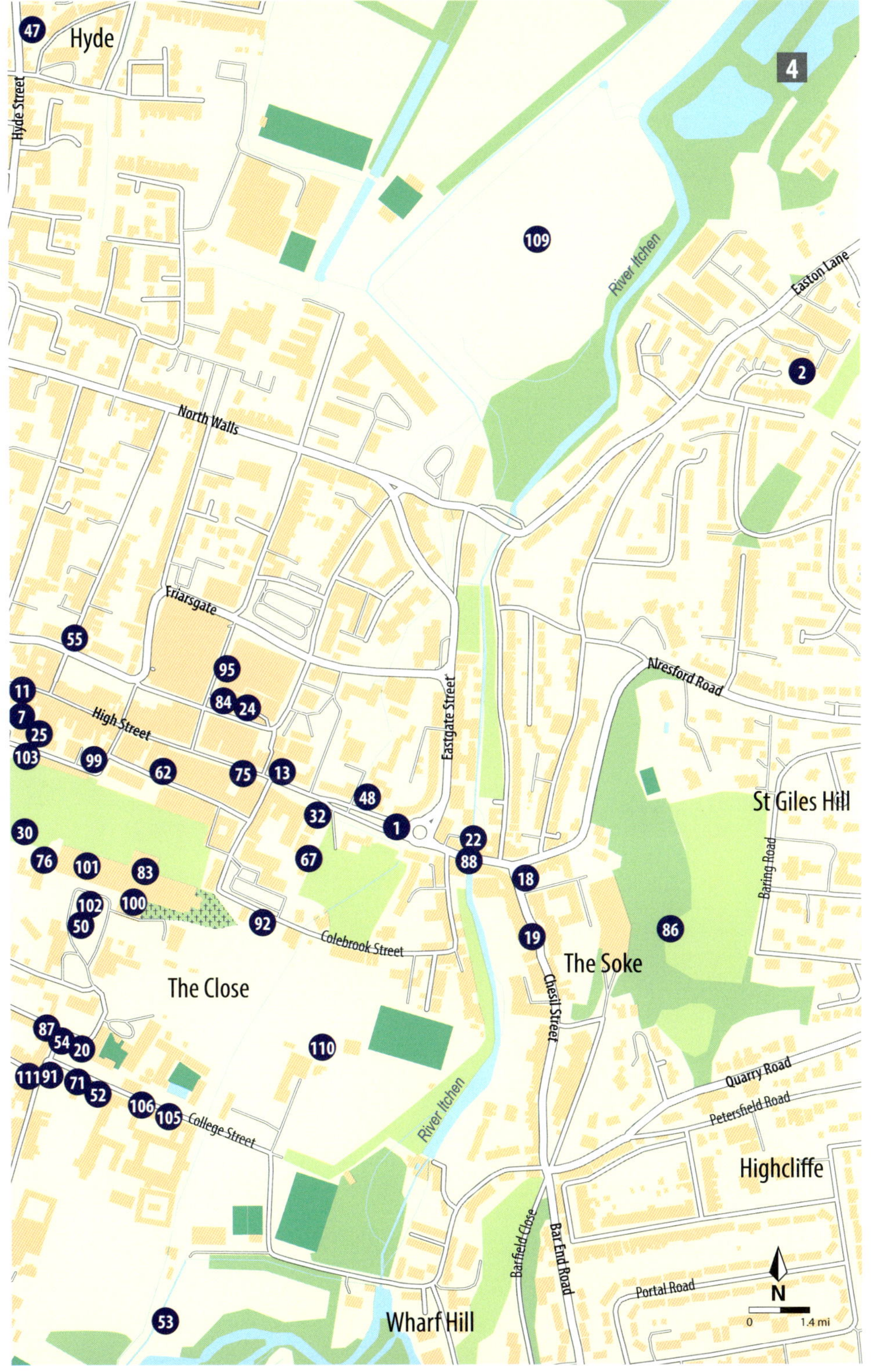
4
Hyde
Hyde Street
47
109
River Itchen
Easton Lane
2
North Walls
Friarsgate
55
95
84
24
11
7
25
103
99
High Street
62
75
13
48
32
1
Eastgate Street
22
88
18
19
Alresford Road
St Giles Hill
Baring Road
30
76
101
83
102
100
50
67
92
Colebrook Street
86
The Soke
Chesil Street
The Close
87
54
20
110
111
91
71
52
106
105
College Street
River Itchen
Quarry Road
Petersfield Road
Highcliffe
Barfield Close
Bar End Road
Portal Road
N
0
1.4 mi
53
Wharf Hill

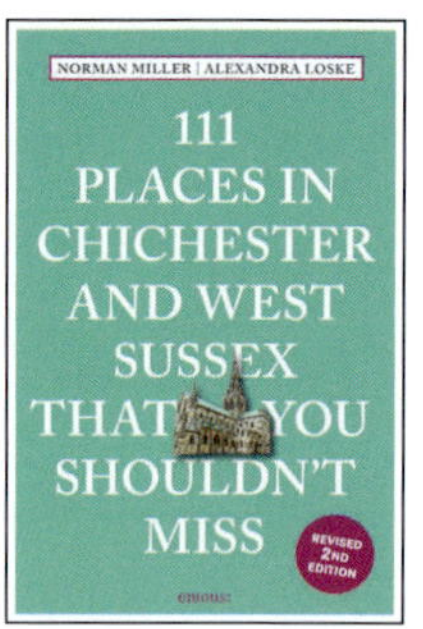

Norman Miller, Alexandra Loske
111 Places in Chichester and West Sussex That You Shouldn't Miss
ISBN 978-3-7408-2807-3

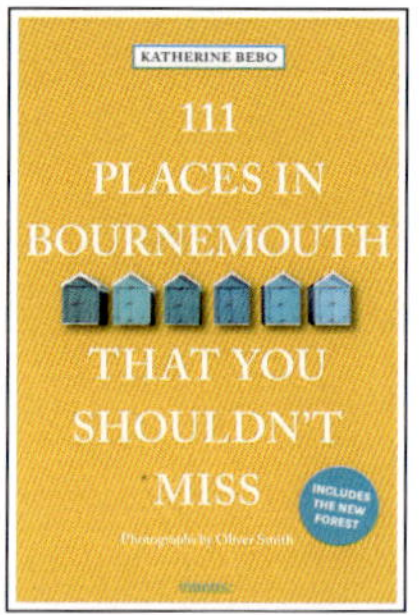

Katherine Bebo, Oliver Smith
111 Places in Bournemouth That You Shouldn't Miss
ISBN 978-3-7408-2646-8

Katherine Bebo, Oliver Smith
111 Places in Poole That You Shouldn't Miss
ISBN 978-3-7408-0598-2

Alexandra Loske
111 Places in Brighton and Lewes That You Shouldn't Miss
ISBN 978-3-7408-1727-5

Karen Heaney, Jeni Bell
111 Places in Dorset That You Shouldn't Miss
ISBN 978-3-7408-2146-3

Catriona Neil, Adrian Spalding
111 Places in Cornwall That You Shouldn't Miss
ISBN 978-3-7408-2805-9

Ed Glinert, David Taylor
111 Places in Yorkshire That You Shouldn't Miss
ISBN 978-3-7408-1167-9

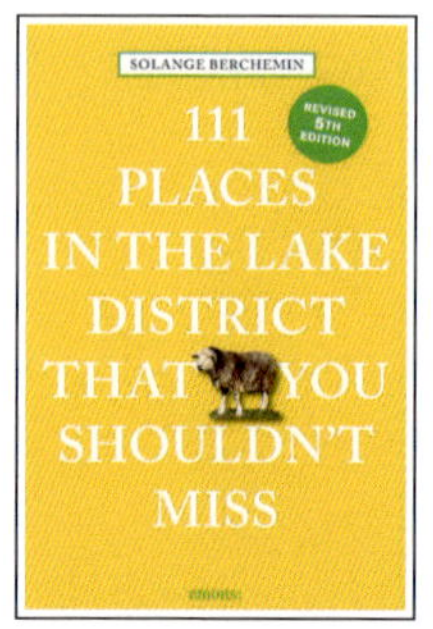

Solange Berchemin
111 Places in the Lake District That You Shouldn't Miss
ISBN 978-3-7408-2824-0

David Taylor
111 Places in Northumberland That You Shouldn't Miss
ISBN 978-3-7408-2923-0

Photo Credits

Gurkha Museum: © The Gurkha Museum Trust
Hampshire Pantry: © Hampshire Pantry
Hattingley Valley: © Hattingley Valley
Highclere Castle: © Highclere Castle
The Ivy Winchester: © The Ivy Winchester
Jane Austen's House: © Jane Austen's House, Chawton; Luke Shears
Jane Austen's Last Home: © Camilla Winter-Moore
Lainston House: © Angela Ward-Brown
Lower Norton Flower Farm: © Lower Norton Flower Farm
Rick Stein: © Rick Stein Winchester
Romsey Abbey: Photo by Anna-Maria Bauer, printed by kind permission of the Vicar and Churchwardens, Romsey Abbey
Sound II: © Winchester Cathedral
Theatre Royal Winchester: © Theatre Royal Winchester
Winchester Bible: © Winchester Cathedral
Winchester Cathedral: © Winchester Cathedral
Winchster Christmas Market: © Winchster Cathedral
Winchester College: © Camilla Winter-Moore
Winchester College Treasury: © Winchester College

Acknowledgements

My heartfelt thanks go to my editor Tania Taylor for her eagle eyes, her encouragement from the first to the last email, and her remarkable patience with me throughout the writing of this book – especially at the end.

I am also deeply grateful to Laura Olk, project manager for the UK and US for Emons, for believing in this project and supporting me at every stage of the process.

My profound thanks go to my partner Steve Barnett for his meticulous proofreading, his unfailing kindness and constant support in all I do. I am especially grateful that he attended Swanwick Writers' Summer School in 2019; it was a chance meeting that changed everything and brought me to this wonderful part of the country.

And, as always, the deepest gratitude goes to my mother Sabine Bauer, who has encouraged my writing as long as I can remember, and to my father Erich Bauer, who is the best business mentor a daughter could wish for.

Thank you also to all the wonderful people I met along the way who shared their projects, stories and knowledge with me: Alison Coleman, Lower Norton Flower Farm; Amy Hickson, Winchester Visitor Information Centre; Amy and Jake, Design Junction; Anna Gammon-Ross, Winchester Science Centre; Barnaby, Tillius; Brian Hayward, Hayward Guitars; Channing Jones, Hattingley Valley; Catherine Fabian, Winchester College; Christine Pullen, Rifleman's Museum; Christopher Harpham, Romsey Abbey; Clive and Tanith Cummings, The Milbury; Colin Bulleid, Royal Hampshire Regiment Trust; Christine Pullen, The Rifleman's Museum; Dan Lloyd, The Railway Inn; David Hazeldine, Char Teas; David Kemp, artist; Debra Valvona Johnson, Hampshire Soap Company; Deryck Newland, Play to the Crowd; Eleanor Dodd, Chesil Rectory; Eleonore Swire, Winchester Cathedral; Emily Millen, Hampshire Pantry; Emma Blyth, Paws For Thought; Emma Boryer, Gurkha Museum; Emma Shaw, The Well Worn; Gary Whiter and Marcus Roe, Cabinet

Rooms; George Orange, street artist; Hannah Gutteridge, Highclere Castle; Hannah Shorthouse, The Old Gaolhouse; Hendog, street artist; Hendrik Engelbrecht, Rick Stein Winchester; Jack Woodgate, Incognito; Janet Theodore, The Hyde Tavern; Jemma Maguire, Winchester Coffee Roasters; Jenny Muncaster and Rachael Alexander, The Colour Factory; Jon Howard, Wykeham Arms; Kate MacLachlan, English Heritage; Kim Simpson, Chawton House; Kristina J. Smith, lino printing artist; Liz Leak, Hampshire Cultural Trust; Lizzie Dunford, Jane Austen's House; Lorraine Estelle, Winchester City Blue Badge & Cathedral Tour Guide; Louise Goodall and Rebecca Hopkins, Mint Tea Boutique; Lyndsay and Nick Butler, Hartley Park Farm; Maria Forsberg, Hotel du Vin Winchester; Marcelo Pugliese, The Old Vine; Mark Horner, South Downs Sourdough; Marzia Colonna, artist; Mike Fowkes, Kinsgate Books & Prints; Neil Wyatt, South Downs Social; Nicolas Roulier, The Ivy Winchester; Nicky and Jon Scott from Owslebury; Paul Riddell, Chesil Theatre; Pippa Sherry, Chocolate Craft; Robert Cole, Letterbox Study Group; Richard Bentley, Watercress Line; Roger Ossa Triviño, The Hospital of St Cross; Sam Carter, Bombay Sapphire; Sam Stones, English Heritage; Sarah Waddington, Lainston House; Sophie Reynold, Jane Austen's House; Sophia Perham, Gilbert White's House & Garden; Steve Haigh, Alfred's Brewery; Steve Scholey, P&G Wells; Sue de Salis, Winchester Tourist Guide; Sue Tapliss, Whitchurch Silk Mill; Tracy Randall, Sir Harold Hillier Garden; Tony Kippenberger, Bishop's Waltham Society; Victoria Burt, Theatre Royal Winchester.

Anna-Maria Bauer is a Hampshire-based journalist, writer and teacher. Originally from Vienna, Austria, she discovered her passion for England while studying at University College London, and has since made the south coast her home.

The information in this book was accurate at the time of publication, but it may change at any time. Please confirm the details for the places you're planning to visit before you head out on your adventures.